AMANDA MUCKALT

THE
STABILITY
EFFECT

Four leadership factors
that will make or break
your organisation

R^ethink

First published in Great Britain in 2024
by Rethink Press (www.rethinkpress.com)

© Copyright Amanda Muckalt

Cover image: Photo by Marcus Woodbridge on Unsplash

For dear Dad and Mum

Norman Muckalt and Pat Muckalt

Contents

Introduction

We are living through one of the greatest global transitions in our lifetimes. No business leader can escape the disruption this brings to the workplace. Economic volatility, the climate crisis and a complex range of geopolitical tensions are leaving people anxious and unsettled. Global health challenges, changes in social values and advances in technology add to the instability of this era.

Organisations that can cultivate stable environments amid this turbulence have a powerful resource to withstand the disruption and respond intelligently to it. Like a boat tacking in stormy waters, a stable organisation can keep moving in its desired direction through the waves of change, influencing the currents as it travels and being influenced by them. Stability gives an organisation a steady platform from which to make the right next move.

In my work with leaders, I've seen their struggle to get stability and change to co-exist and work together in organisations. I've also seen the impact organisations can have in shaping a better world. These two factors inspired me to write this book.

I graduated from university with a first-class honours degree in mathematics. In that world, the importance of maintaining equilibrium around a fixed point as you move forward and evolve was well understood. Applying this principle in the realm of business requires people and systems to continually stabilise around a fixed point as they adapt to their changing environment. With the physicality of an office building becoming less relevant, it's up to you to decide what and where the fixed points in your system are and how you will stabilise around them. Amid all the uncertainty, one thing is certain: strong leadership has never been more important. It's the connectivity that keeps the ship watertight.

At the time of writing, you have a lot of moving parts to deal with. Some people are in the office; others are out of the office. Roles and power dynamics are shifting and the future is unknown. Differing genders, cultures and ages present diverse needs. Relationships are under strain and murmurs of fracture and discontent fill the air. Many people in the workplace have woken up to the freedom and flexibility that exist beyond a traditional office-based work life. The possibility of pursuing personal dreams outside of work now feels within reach. The psychological contract between the organisation and employees is being renegotiated. Some people are leaving. Others are biding their time, waiting for the opportune time to go. Leading a team or an organisation has never been more testing.

At best, these challenges are making things complicated for you as a leader and your organisation. At worst, targets and financial performance are suffering and you feel like you're on the edge, unsupported by your team and unsure how much longer you can go on. Some days you too might be thinking 'I want to do something else. I have a vision and I can't focus on it here because of all these issues going on around me.' Other days, you want to make it work and be part of a great organisation.

On top of this, business decisions are almost impossible to make with any degree of certainty. There are more of them and you are being forced to make them faster amid many unknowns and moving variables. The way forward is rarely clear, but you still feel the pressure to get it right in the eyes of your stakeholders. If you don't make the right choices, say no (or yes) at the crucial moment, choose the right people, identify the key priorities and make the wise investment, then performance suffers. Often, it's hard to know what to do and the best direction to go in. Still, the expectation remains that you'll be decisive, take swift action and drive results.

With the world of work that you grew up in gone, and a barrage of new thinking and jargon to contend with from academics and consultants who don't know your context, it's easy to lose confidence and let self-doubt creep in. However, you can't show it because if people see you're afraid, you'll lose credibility and authority. Leadership can be lonely. You're supposed to have all the answers and others look to you for support. But what about you? Who's got *your* back?

In *The Stability Effect*, I accompany you through a four-part pathway to stability in your organisation that gives you alignment and guides better decision-making. The four parts, which I call IRON and are shown in the table below, make up the four parts of this book.

IRON

Iron is required for life. It ranks in the top five of the earth's most abundant elements yet stands top of the league of nutritional deficiencies in the world. In chemistry, it belongs to the first transition series of elements. Your body needs iron because iron makes haemoglobin, a protein in red blood cells that carries oxygen from the lungs to all parts of the body, and myoglobin, a protein that provides oxygen to muscles. Iron also contributes to the production of some hormones. Without iron, you cannot grow and develop.[1]

Iron is a word that has come to be associated with strength. People 'pump iron' at the gym or swim-cycle-run their way through an Ironman Triathlon to challenge and change themselves. Iron is also associated with smoothing and levelling. You might iron out creases in a garment, or difficulties in a business process.

In *The Stability Effect*, IRON is an acronym that represents the four deep-rooted leadership factors (and the overall pathway) that will make or break your organisation in a world of relentless change.

PART ONE	PART TWO	PART THREE	PART FOUR
Inner Steadiness	Reading The Environment	Overcoming Challenges	Never Done
I	R	O	N

The four-part IRON pathway

With IRON, you strengthen your capacity to stay steady in the stresses of change, read the signals of your environment, move beyond challenges and keep your business (and yourself) moving and evolving, with an inner core that holds you stable.

Once you create stability, you create confidence. People stop feeling agitated and worried about their future, and where they fit into things long-term. The energy in your business can gather and align to deliver your goals.

The leaders I have worked with over the years have increasingly become aware of the importance of their inner game for strong relationships and results. They've realised that the way to create stability around them is to be steady inside themselves and be in a position where they are fulfilling their mission in life. Once they feel that alignment, it cascades throughout the entire workforce.

In a virtuous circle, my courageous clients have stretched and inspired me to go beyond conventional mind-led leadership training, deeper into the inner world of body, breath and energy flows, to create new integrated solutions fit for the chaos and urgency of the times. These new solutions include four pioneering models that acknowledge the whole-personhood of leaders and their teams.

1. My Body-Breath-Mind (BBM) model, which you will learn about in Part One, is a dynamic inner process that recruits the body and the breath as powerful allies alongside the mind, to equip you to access the depth of inner steadiness needed to find balance in rapidly changing conditions.

2. My 'Listen Out, Listen In' process, introduced in Part Two, guides you to read your outer and inner environments with an astuteness that keeps you closely connected with what is happening in your world in real time, so that you can respond with integrity.

3. My 3Cs Team Mobiliser Model, which you will encounter in Part Three, shows you how to use care, communication and collaboration to galvanise your team into aligned action.

4. My 'Vital Five-Element Foundation for Better Decision-Making' is set out in Part Four and gives you a platform from which to continually make aligned decisions so that every choice you make moves you towards a future you want to be part of.

I've worked in the business world for over thirty years. As a chartered accountant and external auditor, I learned about numbers and financial statements. Mergers and acquisitions taught me about deals and the long game. Managing global accounts educated me about sales and matrix structures. However, it wasn't until I led a large and diverse team, and later my own leadership and change business, that I truly understood what makes business work: people who know themselves, care deeply about what they do and make decisions based on what they stand for. They are the oxygen that gives business life.

Whatever else is going on in business, before it becomes about numbers, deals, strategy, structure, process, workspace design and culture, it's about people: who they are, the quality of their choices and actions and their alignment with their deeper self. I've seen a lot of change, but like you, I've never seen change like this.

As you read through the book, I encourage you to proactively engage with the change we're seeing. Make the IRON pathway your own. Use it to create a stability effect that matches you and your business. Highlight everything in the text that resonates. Consider how you are similar and different to the case study characters. Do the awareness exercises at the end of every chapter. Build your IRON Training Programme of practices to take with you at the close of the book.

The Stability Effect supports all areas of life. As you consider how to lead through relentless change at work, know that you can apply the IRON pathway in everyday life to empower and bring positive change to all aspects of your experience. Take it into your leadership, your team, your organisation and your personal life. Tweak it so that it fits your unique context and adds maximum value.

Whether you're a leader of leaders, or a team, by using *The Stability Effect* you can become rock solid, a guiding light in the business, steady in turbulence, able to make wise choices and bring people together with a sense of shared purpose and belonging. Let me show you and your organisation how to not just survive in relentless change, but to thrive and become stronger because of it.

Upon completing *The Stability Effect*, you'll be better equipped to use the potential of change to unite your team, live out what you stand for, deepen your fulfilment and continually shape a better workplace, life and world.

Does that sound good? Well, let's begin.

IRON

PART ONE
INNER STEADINESS

A key reason that you can lose your way in a world of relentless change is that your education and training haven't equipped you to stay inwardly steady without burning out or checking out. Every day a multitude of demands, distractions and people in distress (and excitement) come from all directions and flood your space. It's easy to go into overload or autopilot, simply 'coping' to get through the day and your to-do list, and forget to notice what is going on inside you and how that influences your leadership, decisions, relationships and wellbeing. I want to ensure that you are personally set up for stability right from the off; that you can embrace new attitudes and practices to stay strong inside and be a solid, grounding presence for your team, stakeholders, your decisions and yourself.

The book starts here, with you and your inner steadiness. This part is just as rigorous as the more outward-focused ones to follow. As you read it, you will understand why, and how important your inner game is as a first step towards the broader goals of team and organisational stability. It contains two chapters. The first introduces self-awareness as the foundation of your inner steadiness and dives into what inner steadiness is and what affects it. The second shares tools to help you stay steady in a volatile time that looks set to stay.

ONE
Start With You

'The unexamined life is not worth living.'
—Socrates[2]

Sometimes the best advice is thousands of years old and comes from a context different from our own. Socrates' powerful advocacy of the examined life can be interpreted as suggesting that to be fully human we must examine our lives to help us work out what we should do.

In a similar vein, modern-day leadership experts and researchers flag the importance of gaining self-awareness to realise our full potential. When leaders know themselves, decision-making, relationship-building and business results can benefit. In today's unfamiliar, challenging and boundless world of work, self-awareness could be the most important foundational skill you need to thrive, so we start here, with you, and dive in at the deep end.

This first chapter explores what it means to be a self-aware leader and the importance of this trait to your effectiveness. We excavate inner steadiness, the crucial role it plays in stability, why it's challenging and three of its key reciprocal influences: your perceptions of change, your attitude to learning and your decision-making.

The self-aware leader

I define a self-aware leader as someone who seeks self-knowledge and takes responsibility for what's going on inside them because they understand that their choices and actions can create harm as well as good. Realising the significance of and impact of your inner world on your organisational environment and your leadership motivates you to get to know yourself better without feeling self-indulgent.

Self-awareness is not a fixed state and a self-aware leader is not a finished product. We can be aware in one context and blind in another. We can behave with wisdom and maturity on Monday, and by Friday our inner teenager might be straining to take the reins on our choices.

Given the range of things you deal with day by day, including your own and other people's reactions to change, the more committed you are to knowing yourself and what helps or hinders your steadiness, the better equipped you are to stay steady, and to help your team stay steady, in turbulent times.

It's easy to recognise an absence of inner steadiness in others, and the consequences that follow. You know that the distracted, anxious person who has just rushed out of your office is unlikely to make good decisions today unless they find a way to re-centre. It's obvious. Turning the mirror of awareness onto yourself and seeing clearly what's happening inside you, and how this is reflected in your behaviours, can be somewhat harder.

In her book *Insight*,[3] Dr Tasha Eurich highlights why many senior leaders have blind spots when it comes to their own abilities. One study of more than 3,600 leaders revealed that higher-level leaders significantly overvalue their skills compared with others' perceptions. This might be because senior leaders have fewer people above them who can provide candid feedback, and/or the more power a leader holds the less comfortable people are in sharing their honest experience, in case it hurts their careers. To buck this trend, muster the necessary courage to walk the path of self-awareness. Build safe environments in which your team can be honest with you, seek frequent feedback and learn the art of self-reflection to help you become more self-aware.

Inner steadiness 2.0

Chances are, at your level of responsibility, you already have the capacity to be steady inside. My invitation to you now is to deepen your steadiness to navigate intense volatility and uncertainty, while staying energised, well and able to make necessary decisions and be the role model that keeps your team and wider workforce aligned and motivated. This requires inner steadiness 2.0, where your mind and body are together, aligned and in the present moment. You feel connected and calm inside, comfortable in your own skin and open to your environment.

The traits of inner steadiness 2.0 are especially important in times of turbulence when people look to leadership to hold their environment in as much order as possible in a chaotic world, and to give them guidance, confidence and the courage to stay steady themselves. In uncertainty, even small changes in your emotions or behaviours can affect your team. If you're wobbling, people around you are more likely to wobble. If your thinking is scattered, your team's thinking can become scattered. Decision-making then suffers.

In the IRON pathway, inner steadiness is the crucial foundation that supports the three factors that follow.

Its benefits are vast. Steadiness supports your concentration, focus and clear thinking, your ability to notice what's going on around and within you, and your decision-making. You gain a capacity to maintain a high standard of work even in difficult outer circumstances, build stronger relationships (with others and yourself) and stand your ground while being open to other perspectives. Your wellbeing gets a boost too, because being steady inside helps you manage and contain your energy. You're not easily ruffled by others or the unexpected. A martial artist might call you centred, a yoga expert might describe you as grounded and your team might say you are solid. When you are like this, people enjoy being around you. They feel safe, seen and heard. They trust you to do the right thing even in tricky situations.

Steadiness sets you up to be the leader you want to be.

We all want these benefits, but we face challenges because of the way the human nervous system and psyche work. Under pressure, nervous systems can plunge into unhealthy stress, and react with fight, flight or freeze responses.[4] You then lose connection to your inner steadiness and all its benefits. The same thing happens when you are distracted and not in touch with what is going on inside you for long periods. This is a constant risk in a position of leadership, where your focus is naturally outside of you, tending to your team, stakeholders and shareholders, and dealing with essential business tasks.

Without awareness, losing inner steadiness is an ongoing hazard of your role. Understandably, you might reach the end of a day totally removed from the state of your inner landscape. Your own experience in the present moment can seem irrelevant when you have important stakeholders demanding to see your forecasts for the next twelve months, or annual reports to prepare narrating what has happened in the period just lapsed.

The thing is, reality *is* the present, and your inner world is your barometer. If you don't spend some time there, you don't know how you are or who you are. Unless, of course, there's been a moment when you've lost it, lashed out at someone, made bad decisions or in some other way become aware of an emotional volcano that you had no idea existed. Then, you're even further removed from who you are, but you do know *how* you are, and it's not steady.

Your perceptions of change

Your perceptions of change include your attitudes towards, and interpretations of, change. When you perceive change as a threat, your brain's 'central alarm system' turns this threat into fear. The biochemical reactions that accompany fear affect the steadiness of your body and mind.[5] The more of a threat you experience someone or something to be, the harder it becomes to stay steady.

Being aware of what can set off your inner alarm bells and send you into a reactive state gives you important information for managing your inner steadiness. You might have nerves of steel when dealing with investors who want to pull out of a deal but struggle to keep your cool in conversation with a CTO who is angry about a decision you have made. You may be solid as a rock with a team member who has had some personally devastating news, but despairing when your CFO refuses to listen and shuts down.

Spotting reactions

While it can be tempting to gloss over reactions, or simply not notice them at all in the busyness of your days, spotting them as they arise is key in navigating your experience. Awareness gives you a choice. Learning to recognise the physical, mental, emotional and behavioural signs of a reaction is a subtle but powerful skill to possess in a changing world.

Your body's alarm bell can show as muscles tensing up (for example the jaw, hands, thoracic spine), holding your breath, irregular and/or rapid shallow breathing, stomach upsets, sweaty palms and losing bodily awareness. Mental and emotional sirens include racing thoughts, anger, frustration, despair, feeling nothing, urges to lash out at others or yourself, and impulses to act immediately to get rid of discomfort. Behavioural clues include unhelpful withholding of information, being unable to speak, shouting/speaking too fast or too much, eyes glaring at a computer screen or other people, being impatient and tapping hard on your keyboard.

My habitual signs include tensing my shoulders to 'push through', clenching my teeth to stop myself from speaking out, holding my breath as if waiting for danger to pass and gripping my feet to the ground for support. Emotionally, I doubt myself. Mentally, my thoughts dodge out of my awareness; when I go looking for them, they are usually telling me some version of 'I'm not enough'. Behaviourally, I speed up, packing my days with nonstop activity in an attempt not to feel what has been stirred up.

A client discovered that a build-up of worry about the level of change his business was going through triggered cramps in his arms, and he was holding his breath as he went about his working day. Emotionally, he became frustrated and angry. Behaviourally, he cut himself off from support and became 'invincible'.

If you don't yet know the tell-tale signs of your nervous system in distress, or you're not sure, start increasing your awareness right now. Next time you feel tension and reactivity rising in conversation with someone, in response to an email, social media post, a newspaper or the TV, notice what goes on for you physically, mentally, emotionally and in your actions.

When you're in a reactionary state, it's not the time to make decisions. Old fear-based thinking takes over and governs your choices and actions. The consequence is poor decisions and unwise actions.

Understanding reactions

Having a model or framework to guide your understanding of reactions helps you navigate them and generate more helpful perceptions. There are several available to leaders. We'll look at a couple that I've worked with and know have value. The focus in this chapter is you, but all these models can also be used to help you understand what might be going on with team members and discern how best to deal with that.

David Rock's SCARF model[6] provides a neuroscience-based lens through which to view how you experience change. SCARF details five social factors that activate the same threat and reward responses in your brain that you rely on for physical survival:

- Status (your relative importance to others)

- Certainty (your capability to predict the future)

- Autonomy (your sense of control over events)

- Relatedness (your sense of safety with others)

- Fairness (your perception of fair exchanges between people)

These factors can have a huge influence on how you feel and behave. For the untrained brain, certainty and autonomy are major red flags in times of change when little is certain and systemic complexity can make autonomy feel like a pipedream. Relatedness is under strain because people are more likely to be stressed and there is a lack of daily in-person connection with colleagues. Fairness and status can easily be misjudged in a hybrid world.

In this context, it's easy to see how you may be assessing the modern workplace situation as highly threatening. Left untended, these initial assessments with their associated reactions can create or reinforce ingrained and unhelpful ways of thinking.

A second model is 'The Change Curve', an organisational adaptation of Elisabeth Kübler-Ross's five stages of grief: denial, anger, bargaining, depression and acceptance.[7] These are normal human reactions to loss, and they become relevant in business where life-changing events have an impact on the workforce. The extent to which you experience these stages is unique to you. The aim is to move to acceptance and leverage your full capacity to problem-solve and move forward while healthily processing emotions.

Triggers for safety

We've looked at how your perceptions of threat affect your inner steadiness. To gain a full picture consider too your perceptions of safety. What people, situations and events generate safety for you? These 'glimmers', as they have become known, cue your nervous system to a state of calm.[8]

In an organisation going through a lot of change, glimmers can give you an immediate resource with which to generate steadiness and stability. Finding them is important. They can be as simple as calling a loved one at lunchtime, or taking a few minutes to connect with a friend in the workplace and sharing a moment of laughter or meaning. Whatever it is for you, get to know your glimmers, engage with them and relish them.

It's OK to be a learner

Your attitude to learning affects your ability to reach the depths of inner steadiness required in a context of increasing external instability.

In the Covid-19 pandemic lockdowns, I learned more about learning. My habits at the computer were magnified. Without awareness, I sit with my right shoulder forward. On a leadership embodiment training course,[9] I was reminded of the difference between learning and correction. Noticing that my right shoulder was forward and correcting it into a more aligned position had some uses, but I wasn't learning anything. I was structurally in the right place, but the energy of 'trying' and 'getting it right' that had placed me out of alignment in the first place was still there. The next time I sat at the computer, my right shoulder was in its habitual forward position. It was only by slowing down, exaggerating the out-of-alignment position so that I could truly feel it, then releasing and being with the return towards alignment, that my brain learned a new way to be and my shoulder began to naturally re-align with the rest of my skeleton. I had created connectivity where before there was a disconnect.

For you (and your team), there's a learning journey to go on to create connected and new ways of leading, aligning and deciding in an unstable world. The person who might find that learning most difficult is you. This is understandable, given your position and stage of career. Your team, your clients, your shareholders, the people in your business and the judge in your head can be unforgiving voices in the face of you not knowing, making mistakes and taking time for a learning process instead of pursuing the immediate results of a correction (without learning).

'I have to know the answer' could have been a core belief that propelled you into a position of leadership. It's not just you. Alison Gopnik is a professor of psychology and philosophy at the University of California, Berkeley, where she runs the Cognitive Development and Learning Lab. Author of over a hundred papers and half a dozen books, including *The Philosophical*

Baby,[10] Alison takes the minds of children seriously. A child's mind is tuned to learn. Alison calls children the R&D departments of humanity. She explains that a mind tuned to learn works differently from a mind trying to exploit what it already knows, which is what most adults do. The older we get, the harder it is for us to learn, to question, to reimagine because of the way our brains change as we age.[11]

The truth is that in your role as a leader, you are expected to know the answer – and fast. The resolution here ultimately lies in a paradigm shift in the organisational and wider stakeholder culture that allows leaders to not know the answer immediately. In the meantime, you can proactively nurture helpful attitudes for learning. These include curiosity, discovery and flexibility. Kindness towards yourself helps too because it creates safety, and we learn best when we feel safe. None of us has had to deal with this level of change before. Can you permit yourself to learn? It helps to know that learning isn't about fixing yourself. There's nothing wrong with you. It's simply a case of learning how to access and bring forth new skills.

How do *you* make decisions?

The decisions you make have an impact on your inner steadiness (and vice versa). Or, to put it another way, the Stability Effect generates and relies on a high quality of decision-making. Every day you make hundreds of decisions. Many are automatic. The alarm clock goes off, you lean over and put it on snooze, or you switch it off and leap up. That's a decision made before you're even out of bed. By the time you've left the house, or sat yourself down at your home workstation, you will have made at least a dozen more: cleaning your teeth, getting dressed, putting the kettle on. You don't have to consciously decide to do these things. While no thought or active decision-making is required, they are decisions nonetheless. Automatic decision-making is necessary. Can you imagine what life would be like if every morning you woke up and had to consciously work through the process of what to do next?

The more deliberate decisions you make include how to structure your day, when to answer emails and how to approach a particular task. Business decisions involve the people you need in your team for it to excel, the profit you require to run a viable business, the priorities this year to deliver your strategy, the processes you need for effective operations, the projects you will and will not invest in, the initiatives you'll authorise for employee wellbeing and many more.

Almost all our decisions affect others. The ones you make in your leadership role can affect hundreds and thousands of people, so it's important that you understand your process, explain your decisions, defend them and stand by them.

We each have a default approach to making decisions that reflects what we've learned from others as we've grown up, societal norms and our personality. It might be years, or even decades, since you put the spotlight on your decision-making. To revisit now amid the ongoing intense changes in the world of work could stand you apart. It helps you choose to be the conscious explorer (not the unconscious exploiter) that the world and your workplace so desperately need.

Investing in a personality profiling assessment will give you a wealth of information to increase your understanding of yourself and your leadership, and can help you make better decisions. Many such profiling tools are readily available online, for example, Gallup's CliftonStrengths, Myers-Briggs and DiSC. You can always debate the accuracy of psychometrics but their ability to start useful lines of enquiry to increase self-knowledge is second to none.

When you understand your approach and attitude to decision-making, your appetite for risk and uncertainty, whether you are generally a hasty or hesitant decision-maker and your decision-making strengths and weaknesses, you can counteract the pitfalls in your style and magnify your strengths. For example, factual personality types who tend to dismiss groundbreaking but unproven potential in a situation might benefit by allowing possibility into their decision-making process. More imaginative types who don't rely on evidence and can dismiss important facts could benefit from a sobering reality check. A hasty decision-maker may choose to slow down their process, while a hesitant person may consciously choose to speed it up. Whatever the type of decision you are facing or the components of your decision-making style, being aware puts you in a position of strength.

CASE STUDY: Ingrid has lost her steadiness and doesn't know what she needs

Ingrid is a partner in a law firm specialising in employment law. Academically brilliant, she excelled at school and university and was promoted ahead of her peer group. Ingrid has a strong sense of right and wrong. Always knowing the answer has got her to where she is today, but the pandemic threw her. Rising enquiries from panicked employers and employees in unknown situations left her mentally over-stimulated. As her mind raced around searching for novel solutions to new problems and seeking stability in the face of spiralling uncertainty, without realising it she became more and more distracted and disconnected from her body and feelings.

Things have continued to be incredibly busy for Ingrid; she's often irritable at work and frequently expects to drop a major ball or become ill. She finds one member of her team infuriating and is worried that one day soon she will really lose it with him. Naturally risk-averse, Ingrid is biding her time with some key decisions relating to staff numbers and the strategic direction of the business. Her nervous system hasn't recovered from pandemic stress. Holidays merely scratch the surface of her exhaustion. Ingrid realises she doesn't know what she needs to get her inner composure back. We'll reconnect with Ingrid at the end of Chapter 2 to see how she resolved her predicament.

CHAPTER EXERCISE: Starting points for your self-awareness

To begin working on your self-awareness, reflect on the following:

- What three situations challenge your inner steadiness?
- What three words describe your attitude to learning?
- What three things are you good at in decision-making?

Summary

Your self-awareness is essential to leading in relentless change. As you step onto the IRON pathway towards stability in your organisation, you should:

- Acknowledge that your choices and actions can create both harm and good

- Understand that inner steadiness arises when your mind and body are aligned and in the present moment

- Know what situations you perceive as threatening and disrupt your inner steadiness

- Know also what creates safety

- Recognise you're a learner too and be OK with that

- Spotlight how you make decisions

TWO
Balancing Act

'Do you pay regular visits to yourself?'
—Rumi[12]

Have you ever done squats on a bosu ball? Or, even harder, on an upside-down bosu ball, with its domed surface resting on the ground and your feet on the flat base? If you have, you'll know the challenge of it. To move on the wobbling platform beneath your feet with any degree of balance and poise, you must connect internally and get into your core. Lose focus for a second and you're either falling off the ball or working hard to get back to equilibrium. Leading a team and a business in an unstable world can feel a lot like this.

In this chapter, we look at how you can stay steady in this volatile terrain by strengthening your connection to yourself. Techniques include finding a balance between being and doing, holding healthy boundaries, knowing what you stand for, applying my BBM model and discovering personal practices for ongoing steadiness that work for you.

Being and doing

Until recently, I hadn't thought about Silas Marner since English literature classes in school. The previous weeks I'd been head down, working hard, writing my book and focusing on what was needed to meet a publishing deadline. To my dismay, I was losing the joy in my writing. Breaks had become mere refuel stops. No joy there either. Sharing my predicament with a friend, he pointed out my resemblance to George Eliot's famous character Silas Marner.[13] Only, instead of being locked in a room with the monotony of a loom and the repetition of the task at hand, I was locked in a room with my computer, my keyboard and my approaching deadline.

Recognition of my reality was enough to release me from the joyless jam I'd gotten myself into. Breaks from the screen became real breaks. The summer months gave me a garden in bloom, allowing me to be with myself and vibrant colour in a nourishing way. Ten minutes out of the house and in conscious presence with nature, with feet on the earth and hands idle or cradling rose heads, brought me back into balance. Inwardly steady, replenished and ready for the next encounter with my book and computer, I could go back inside and re-engage my 'doing' mode.

Think about your past week. What was the balance of your being and doing? We're not looking for 50:50 perfection here. That would be unrealistic, given your role and responsibilities, and probably your aspirations too. What we're looking for is a balance that supports your vitality and capacity to stay steady, to lead and to make wise decisions in demanding and changing times. I think it's one of the biggest challenges of a pressured leadership role: remembering you are a human being as well as a human doing.

DAILY PRACTICE: Stillness

To bring more beingness into your world, adopt a stillness practice each day. Meditation is one example. It's learnable and evidence-based,[14] and so a reliable place to start. Sitting quietly and focusing on your breath or an object for even five minutes a day can be beneficial. If meditation isn't for you, take a daily mindful walk, or stroke your pet on breaks or at the end of your working day and be fully present in the experience.

Boundaries matter

A river needs banks to flow. When it floods and bursts beyond them, all the energy in the water that was once channelled into a powerful current is dispersed and lost. The banks give the river a boundary, a container that holds its energy and generates stability and safety.

In your leadership role, healthy boundaries with yourself and with others support you to be steady inside. Boundaries with yourself might be closing the door (physically or metaphorically) on the tasks of the day, going to bed an hour earlier than usual to recover from a busy spell, sticking to a social media curfew after 8pm and spending time with family or friends on Saturdays instead of working. Boundaries can also apply to the thoughts you let into your mind. You're in charge. Be discerning about what you watch, read and listen to. Imagine your thought processes as being a river of clean water. The moment you let someone (and it could be you) put a drop of ink in that river, everything changes.

Boundaries with others might mean refusing to engage in idle banter or getting pulled into a drama that isn't your business or business-related. This can be especially tricky if you're new in the role and shifting previously established relationship dynamics, such as becoming the boss of a former peer. Holding healthy boundaries with others isn't about a lack of care and compassion; that can lead to disconnection from people and becoming an isolated leader. It's about being able to say no with kindness and managing your energy.

Stay alert to what's going on without absorbing any destructive emotional charge circulating around you. I once asked a client what was clouding her vision. The question stopped her in her tracks. 'Everyone else's drama,' she replied. Client work has shown me that managing your energy not only keeps you steady inside with all the associated benefits that has, but it also boosts your motivation and performance. Some questions to ask yourself to raise your awareness about how you manage your energy include: What do I let into my energy? What do I refuse entry? What energy do I cultivate inside me? What energy do I let go of? How do I recharge my energy?

DAILY PRACTICE: Boundaries review

Review your boundaries daily and keep them healthy by asking two simple questions:

- How were my boundaries today?
- What will I do differently tomorrow?

What do you stand for?

What impact does this question have on you? Responses can vary from a visceral strengthening that is felt in the body and creates a strong open posture and confident mindset, through the neutral ground of ambivalence, to a weakening effect of body contraction and a mindset of doubt and worry.

At the time of writing, we've all been through a lot of disruption. Where has it left you? Do you know, with a firm conviction, what you stand for now?

For me, what you stand for refers to the bigger picture of your identity, beyond the small stuff. It's about who you are. It isn't an intellectual exercise. It shows up in your actions and the way you live and lead. When you are rooted in what you stand for you are solid as a rock, an expression of inner steadiness 2.0. This can apply to both personal and organisational identity.

Leaders and organisations make use of a broad range of identity markers to express what they stand for. These include values, core beliefs, guiding principles, purpose, mission and vision. The most common ones I come across are values, purpose and vision. Whatever language and nomenclature you choose to adopt, when these descriptors are authentic, they go hand in hand with strong inner steadiness and guide decisions, direction and behaviours. When they don't work well, they are empty words. A false promise. In organisations, they hang bereft on office walls or dress up emails with fictitious meaning. People cannot feel them in their core. They look to the floor when they are mentioned or roll their eyes skywards in exasperation.

When you (and your organisation) lose touch with what you stand for and you don't know who you are, you put yourself on a slippery slope. Before long, you end up living a life that is not your own, feeling out of sorts or deeply unfulfilled.

The more senior you are in business, the more essential it becomes to have alignment between your personal and organisational identity. If what you stand for and what your business stands for are at odds, you're in trouble. It's hard to be steady inside when every day you go to work in a business that holds a different set of values to you and is heading south when you're going north. Leaders must stay grounded in what they stand for. You can find immediate strength when you reconnect to this and remind yourself of why you became a leader in the first place.

> **DAILY PRACTICE: Connecting with what I stand for**
>
> Connect with what you stand for every day in a way that works for you. Keep a visual reminder beside your computer; have an auditory reminder through a recorded memo of your own words; find a felt sense by tuning in and knowing what your body feels like when you are acting with purpose, facing your true north and honouring your values.

Finding inner steadiness with BBM

Inner steadiness is a dynamic experience, not a rigid state. Throughout every day you will go in and out of balance. That's not the problem. The problem arises when you don't notice what's going on; when you get hooked into an unhelpful narrative; when you stay out of balance, or squash your emotions to get through without later processing them.

When I begin working with leaders, most of them already know how to self-regulate and master their emotions for steadiness. If this is you, be curious for a moment and ask yourself: 'In the process of mastering my emotions, have I cut off from my own heart, my joy, my capacity to feel compassion and passion?'

Leaders are trained to present a calm and steady exterior at work, no matter what is going on. After all, you can't panic and shout 'Help! What should we do?' when the unexpected happens. Inside, though, when faced with challenges and pressures, there might be a much more complex and unseen picture going on, like the proverbial swan swimming serenely across a lake while its legs paddle away ten to the dozen beneath the surface.

Outwardly, you might calmly advise your team how to respond to the unpredicted and high-stakes news, but inwardly you could be experiencing feelings of dread, anger or anxiety. You might already be in the worst-case scenario, or berating yourself that you should have spotted this, replaying the precise moment when there was a clue that it could happen and you were too busy to follow up. While it's the right call to keep this from your team, if you keep your inner world from yourself for any length of time, you will lose connection to what's going on for you. Those kicking swan legs, which might be your racing thoughts or churning stomach, can lead to you burning out and checking out. Is the way you've learned to be steady making you ill?

The Body-Breath-Mind model

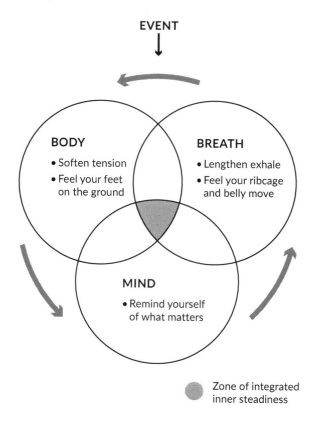

EVENT

BODY
• Soften tension
• Feel your feet
  on the ground

BREATH
• Lengthen exhale
• Feel your ribcage
  and belly move

MIND
• Remind yourself
  of what matters

Zone of integrated
inner steadiness

The BBM model is a dynamic inner process I've developed that returns you to steadiness in the moment when you've lost balance so that you can respond to events, people, dilemmas and decisions calmly and without reactivity. It also incorporates reflection time after the event, where you give yourself the space to process your experience in a contained and structured way. This means you can learn from it and make better choices next time. The reflection doesn't have to take long. Just a few minutes can make a difference and ensure you are not storing up problems that affect your leadership and wellbeing further down the line.

I developed BBM because most of the advice for leaders to stay steady in pressured situations is mind-led and doesn't invite awareness of the body, deepening enquiry and transformation. I've observed that mind-only approaches have limited lasting impact in cultivating ongoing steadiness and a responsiveness fit for the challenges of the times. BBM introduces a holistic and longer-term approach. It includes the body (because experiences of 'threat' and 'safety' live in the body) and the breath as essential allies of the mind, and it incorporates reflection. It's more than self-regulation and mindfulness, although it includes both. An apt word to describe the principles it embodies might be 'wholeness'.

The aim of BBM is not to transform you into a flatline leader. It's to help you reduce reactivity so that you can stay steady in your leadership and be able to make responsive choices.

DAILY PRACTICE: BBM in the moment

To reap the rewards of BBM, adopt it as a practice. As soon as you notice that you're being knocked off balance in your working day, by your own or other people's reactivity, bring your attention to your body and breath instead of cutting yourself off from both.

Whether you are standing, sitting or moving:

- Soften areas of tension in your body and feel your feet on the ground
- Lengthen your exhale, breathe gently through your nose and feel your breath move your ribcage and belly as you engage your diaphragm
- Remind yourself of what matters to you (your purpose, a value, your intention in the specific situation you are in) and orient around that

Your mind might want to pull you into patterns of unhelpful thinking. Acknowledge that and let the story go. Firmly but kindly tell your mind you'll return to it later to explore the thinking and emotion involved in losing balance.

All this might sound a lot. In the moment it can take one to three seconds. These seconds are the difference between you lashing out at someone or lashing in at yourself, and the considered response that can arise when you connect to your body and breath in the first instance.

DAILY PRACTICE: BBM reflection

BBM in the moment partners with a reflective practice for optimum effectiveness. Just like iron is essential in the production of steel, reflection is essential for consistent inner steadiness in turbulent times.

As a leader, sometimes it's necessary to shut down feelings in the moment to get things done. If you don't later process them and release them, you end up with accumulated tension. It's not dealing with feelings that creates instability.

Give yourself space each day to reflect on what has affected your inner steadiness, and what helps and hinders you to stay steady. For those experiences where you lost steadiness and drew on BBM in the moment (or wish you had), return to them and take a closer look. If it's not possible to pause during the day, set aside a few minutes at the end of the day to remember and review.

Use a practical six-step modification of the BBM sequence suitable for reflection as follows.

1. **Breath.** Settle your breathing into a 'slow and low' rhythm where you can feel the breath in your lower ribcage and belly.

Most of us breathe too fast. Research has shown the optimum number of breaths at rest is eight to twelve per minute.[15] This might seem impossible at first read, but with practice, you can do it. Inhale for two to three seconds, exhale for three to four seconds and pause for two to three seconds before initiating the next inhalation.

2. **Facts.** Recall the facts of what happened. Take up the observer position and state the events as they happened without interpretation or assumption.

3. **Feelings.** Recall your feelings at the time and name them without judgement.

If you find it difficult to name feelings, you're not alone. For most busy professionals, it's not been part of our education, or work experience to date. A 'feelings wheel' can help you expand your emotional language. This benefits you and your team as your capacity to identify their emotions increases too. The wheel below is my adaptation of Dr Gloria Willcox's 'The Feeling Wheel'.[16] It shows seventy-two feelings organised around six primary feelings: sad, scared, mad, strong, joyful and calm.

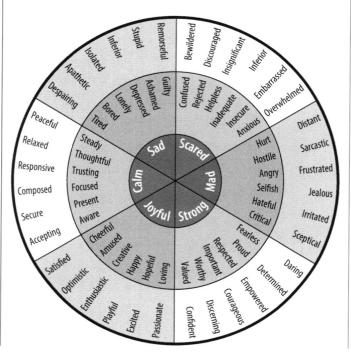

The feelings depicted in the wheel are not a complete overview of all possible feelings. They serve as a starting point to help you describe your emotional experience.

There's no need to analyse your feelings. Dr Tasha Eurich's research for *Insight* showed that asking ourselves why we feel what we feel is unlikely to elicit helpful answers.[17] It's the naming of feelings that relaxes our nervous system so that we can receive their message and release them. Think of it as a practice to build awareness in the moment. Over time, you'll be able to name feelings when they arise.

4. **Thoughts.** Some questions to guide reflection about your thinking processes include:

- What was your mental narrative at the time you lost your steadiness?
- Is your narrative true?
- If it is, what is the evidence for this?
- Who are you as a leader when you believe the narrative?
- Who would you be without it?
- How would you feel if you didn't believe it?
- How else can you perceive the situation?
- What possibilities open up for you, others and the world as you choose a more helpful narrative?
- What can you learn here?

5. **Body.** Turn your attention to your body. Can you remember the physical experiences that accompanied your thoughts and feelings? Acknowledge what they were and notice how your body is now.

> 6. **Choice.** Finally, and importantly, you reach the point of reflection: choice.
>
> Given your learnings and insights, what will you choose to do differently tomorrow or the next time a similar situation occurs?

Working with BBM enhances the quality of your thoughts, your breath and the way you stand, sit and move. It helps you healthily process emotions and think clearly without old conditioning getting in the way. Your words, tone of voice and body language hold the invitation of connection (with others and yourself) rather than disconnection. You're also open to the people and space around you. This openness is a strong foundation from which to read the environment, which we'll be looking at in Part Two.

Continued application of BBM expands your zone of integrated inner steadiness. You learn to centre within swiftly, amid the most challenging circumstances, and genuinely react less, rather than not reacting simply because you're cut off from your feelings.

Day-to-day practices

While at my first appointment with a physiotherapist, I was describing what I had been doing to alleviate neck pain. She patiently listened to me and then asked 'Is it working?' No, it wasn't working. I'd been doing it anyway, in the hope that something would change, unconsciously thinking it was better than nothing. The reality is the wrong approach could have been aggravating the problem. This experience reminded me of the importance of thinking like a scientist, testing out potential solutions to problems and tweaking as required, until we find what works.

Think like a scientist to find practices that work for you in establishing, maintaining and deepening your inner steadiness. Then stick with them. Practice means doing something regularly so that you can do it better or change a behaviour. Everyone is different. What works for you might not work for a team member, and vice versa.

WEEKLY PRACTICE: Taking my body to work

We've mentioned inner steadiness practices already in the four areas of focus of this chapter: being and doing, boundaries, what you stand for and BBM.

There is a further inner steadiness practice on my website called Taking My Body To Work that homes in on your physical body at work. Go to https://centrefornewleadership.com/tmbtw to find out more.

Practices are important in the IRON pathway and each part of the book offers you relevant suggestions.

When you've completed the book, the My IRON Training Programme section allows you to build a personalised practice action plan to keep *The Stability Effect* alive in your life and leadership.

CASE STUDY: Ingrid reclaims her steadiness

Let's return to Ingrid to see how she reclaimed her inner steadiness. A rare moment of reflection prompted Ingrid to take a full day out of her busy schedule to break the momentum she was being carried along by. She knew she needed to reconnect to herself and make some changes. Feeling too wired to sit and relax for long enough to mentally work things out, she walked the coastal path. As she set out, she remembered why she was doing the work she was doing and what truly mattered to her. Then she reflected on the past six months. For the first time, she acknowledged the emotion she'd been holding in. She named what she'd been feeling: sad about the staffing situation; anxious about the future; overwhelmed by the ongoing uncertainty. She let herself cry and felt the tension fall from her body. As she walked, her strength returned. She became aware of the power in her legs, and her shoulders relaxed. She began to think more clearly and realised how entangled she had become with her infuriating team member.

She committed to three key practices that day and followed through on all of them: consciously applying BBM in the moment when she felt tensions rise; spending a few minutes every evening reviewing her boundaries; and using a feelings wheel to name the feelings that had come up for her in the day, irrespective of whether she'd felt reactive. Three weeks after her day on the coast, Ingrid was already feeling the benefit of her practices.

Ingrid, like many of us, had become habitually off balance. Her reconnection day brought her back in touch with the bigger picture of her life, her body and her feelings, and she maintained her inner steadiness through her three chosen practices.

CHAPTER EXERCISE: Just 10 minutes, Part One

Sit (or walk) for just 10 minutes at the end of each day, for three consecutive days, and reflect on:

- Three feelings you've experienced during the day
- Three words that best describe what it's been like being in your body
- Three actions your wisest self invites you to take tomorrow in response to your new awareness

You can make this exercise a practice by doing it on an ongoing basis.

Summary

To be steady inside as you move through the pressures and challenges of your day is a dynamic balancing act. To stay in balance:

- Remember the importance of being as well as doing

- Maintain healthy boundaries

- Stay connected with what you stand for

- Apply the BBM model in the moment when you are knocked off balance to steady you, and later reflect on the experience to process and learn

- Adopt practices to support your inner steadiness

IRON

PART TWO
READING THE ENVIRONMENT

Now that you have what you need to find, maintain and deepen your inner steadiness without burning out or checking out, we turn our attention outwards to your team and organisation. Hybrid workspaces, a multigenerational workforce, accessing talent, diversity equity and inclusion and artificial intelligence are just some of the big issues that pose new questions regarding an organisation's capacity to make wise choices for a sustainable future.

Chapter 3, the first chapter in Part Two, focuses on the implications of this changing landscape for your leadership; the growing significance of reading the environment, building a learning culture and nurturing a sense of belonging; and the decision-making of you and your team. Chapter 4 guides you to build new skills to help you read your new environment so that you can respond to it with integrity.

THREE

The Changing Landscape

'They must often change who would be constant in happiness or wisdom.'
—Confucius[18]

The EY Future Workplace Index analysed responses from C-suite leaders at 501 companies across industry sectors, ranging from 250 employees to more than 25,000, and concluded that 'the future is hybrid'.[19] Their research revealed that 87% of companies say that the pandemic has changed the role of the office for their business. What was once the central hub of connection is now fragmented for many organisations. Some might say a hybrid workplace was coming anyway, alongside technology changes and a workforce with rapidly evolving needs, but few would dispute that Covid-19 has slammed its foot down hard on the accelerator of change, leaving organisations (and their leaders) to deal with the consequences.

The changing workplace landscape brings with it both challenge and opportunity. How this situation is managed is crucial. You and your team have an important role in learning to think, feel, want, know, choose and do what is right for now and what will influence future circumstances for the greater good. The present chapter explores your leadership in this changing landscape; the rising significance of reading the environment; the importance of a learning culture and sense of belonging; and the decision-making by you and your team.

New leadership

Leadership is undergoing huge change in a world of work where turbulence and disruption are the norm. When your future is fundamentally unknown and the needs of teams and employees are in constant evolution, there are exciting opportunities for changes in leadership attitudes and actions. An era of global transition calls for an era of new leadership. Mindsets of possibility, partnership and discovery have never been more important than they are at this moment in organisational history. At the same time, successfully navigating such changed and changing landscapes challenges your self-confidence, good judgement and ability to learn. Without stability, the whole pack of cards can come crashing down. Your role as a leader is to hold the seemingly opposing forces of stability and change in a dynamic balance that allows the organisation and employees to thrive.

Consultancies, think tanks and academics are producing inspiring white papers about leading in this time. While you can learn from them, it's wise to start where you, your team and your organisation are. If you introduce something too countercultural it can destabilise your business and backfire. The skill is in discerning what can be introduced while maintaining a stable platform for growth. Think evolution rather than revolution if you want dynamic stability.

Reading the environment

Evolution and reading the environment go hand in hand. Reading the environment means noticing and accurately interpreting the significance of what's happening in your team, business, market and yourself. It's about awareness in real time and is critical in changing conditions when you can't rely on what has come before as a useful indicator of what is to come.

Reading the environment sets you up to do two distinct but related things: make the micro choices for growth that arise every day and have immediate impact; and make the big, longer-term decisions for the maturation of you and your business. When you read the environment well, you put out fires before there's a problem; spot opportunities, identify decisions needed and make wise choices; do what is right for now and what moves you towards the results you want in the future. Done badly, you miss important cues that have an impact on people and performance and make poor choices at the wrong time that lead you in the wrong direction and destabilise your whole system. These are important contrasts to acknowledge. Yet reading the environment is rarely binary and it isn't about perfection; it's an ongoing process that relies on learning.

The importance of a learning culture

Learning fast in uncertain, changing and hybrid realities is a priority of our times. Yet real learning requires a certain slowness. How can we square this circle? There are a few principles to consider in building a learning culture that can hold the paradox of learning fast and slow.

First, the sheer rate of change means that we must be deliberate in our learning effort, and continually challenge assumptions. Every organisation and leader should be asking the question 'How are we learning?' Without a proactive and clear learning strategy in place, the opportunity that this time in history presents will slip through our fingers. This strategy must include reflective practice.

Reflective practice

We introduced reflective practice concerning the BBM model in Chapter 2. As well as a tool to strengthen your inner steadiness, reflection supports your broader capacity as a leader who needs to learn quickly in rapid change.

Reflective practice isn't new. It was first put on the learning map in 1984 by learning theorist David Kolb in his creation of the learning cycles.[20] Many psychologists and educators have since refined his reflection framework, notably researcher Graham Gibbs in 1988 with his six-stage reflective cycle.[21] Models of reflection are based on the premise that experience alone does not necessarily lead to learning. Deliberate reflection on our experiences helps us extract meaning from those experiences and use them to learn, develop and take informed action.

What is new is the urgency of the application of the learning gained through reflection. Fresh information is coming at you thick and fast right now. More people than ever demand your time, and the decisions piled up in front of you are all important. It's almost impossible to process your experiences and extract key learnings in the moment. Reflective practice adds real value for you here, as taking the time to learn and think translates into considered action. While you may feel there are more pressing things to spend your time on, once you commit to a regular reflective practice, your awareness can soar and learning deepen, both personally and organisationally. The message for leaders today is loud and clear: time out to reflect will give time back to you.

Second, we must address the neurological challenges of adult learning, which we discussed in Chapter 1. These are made worse by a business and economic culture that prizes efficiency and dismisses play, a known enabler of learning.[22]

Finally, we need to start paying close attention to what is happening now and move in real time to support our read of the environment. This can be hard for outcome-focused businesses with an eye on the finish line and one step ahead.

Amy Edmondson, Novartis Professor of Leadership and Management at the Harvard Business School and a leading thinker in the building of learning environments in the modern business world, suggests that the best conditions for learning happen when there is high psychological safety and high accountability. I would add to this a sense of belonging, too.

Psychological safety

For an individual at work, psychological safety is a belief that they will not be punished or humiliated for speaking up with ideas, questions, concerns and mistakes. It describes a person's perceptions about the consequences of taking interpersonal risks in their work environment. Building environments of psychological safety through your example, and agreed standards of behaviour within your team, allows people to be open without fear of repercussion.

You are much more likely to find out what's going on around you and gather important information for decisions when team members can drop any pretence that they've got it all sorted and know all the answers. You can't read a closed book. An environment that is cloudy with secrets and unspoken truths is hard to read.

Your behaviour has a key impact on the psychological safety of your team. Signs that there is psychological safety include team members speaking up about concerns and mistakes, actively seeking feedback from you and asking for help when they need it.[23]

Accountability

Healthy accountability within a person means that they want to take responsibility for their actions because they care about what they do. It isn't about taking responsibility because they fear the consequences of not doing so. The way you lead and support your team affects how accountable they feel.

As you build a hybrid learning culture, another question to ask is 'How can we maintain consistently high psychological safety and accountability?' Things can go south quickly in environments of change and the heightened fear that often accompanies them. Safety deteriorates, the survival instinct kicks in and it can become all about 'me and my world'. Watch out for your team pulling apart rather than together. Leadership teams can be particularly at risk. There is an ever-present temptation to focus on protecting and defending the function they lead at the expense of collaborative firmwide initiatives. However, any team where safety becomes an issue is vulnerable. The inbuilt mindset of competition that many high achievers have can become unhealthy, creating issues in alignment, decision-making and stability of the whole.

A sense of belonging

A sense of belonging gives you and your team intrinsic stability and a feeling of connection with each other that positively affects safety, accountability, learning and the ability to read the environment.

Do people in your team feel like they belong? What impact have the pandemic and subsequent workplace changes had on them? Do you know? Have you asked them? How steady are they feeling? Where are they with the five social factors of the SCARF model and The Change Curve that we explored in Chapter 1? Instead of complicated wellbeing packages, take the time to ask people questions about how they are.

In 2019, a Harvard Business Review article recounted an EY survey where more than 40% of US respondents reported feeling physically and emotionally isolated in the workplace.[24] And that was *before* the pandemic. The survey pointed to one simple solution: establish more opportunities for colleagues to check in with one another. Feeling connected with others in the organisation reflects the human need to belong to something greater than ourselves. We need to find community, people who resonate with and value us. Then we share information, skills and ourselves.

In *Belonging*, Owen Eastwood describes a tribal process where the tribe leader has three stones, each representing a core value of the tribe. The leader sits in a circle with their team and picks up one stone at a time and gives it meaning throughout the story. The leader then hands each stone to a team member, who holds it, feels it and explains what the value represented by that stone means to them, before passing it to the next person. In this way, every value comes to life and has personal meaning for all team members. The stones and the process become a powerful symbol of team belonging and connection with the community values.[25]

To strengthen belonging in your team, have a conversation with them about the core values of your business. Show leadership by sharing meaningful stories about what each of the values means for you, and then with the business. Let all team members do likewise.

The values exercise connects your team and can give you, as the leader, a much-needed boost to your sense of belonging. Sometimes when you have a job that is high status and carries a lot of responsibility, you can lose that sense of being part of something bigger. Of course, the reverse can happen too. You might realise that those stones and the values they represent mean nothing to you anymore, and no longer align with what you stand for. The exercise will take on a different, more personal meaning for you then.

How do you and your team make decisions?

Old frameworks, tools, skills and attitudes that worked in more stable times don't work as well in dynamic conditions and an environment of increasing interconnectedness. Many businesses, leaders and their teams are scratching their heads, wondering how they can automate decision-making to save time without losing that quality that can only come from relational, deliberate thinking and conscious ongoing evaluation of choices.

Adopting the right approach to making a decision is important. You can experiment a bit when the decision is low-risk, but high-risk decisions require more confidence to make. One bad choice with significant consequences can have a devastating effect.

It's easy for decision-making to become fractured in changing times. Challenges around timing, relevancy of data gathered and a collective obsession with reaching an end point can leave leaders with a huge headache. Making decisions brings about change and sets direction, but they could be outdated by the end of the week. Not making them means handing over agency and being swept along by external conditions in a rapidly changing world. If you decide on something too fast, due to external pressures, you risk making a poor decision. If you decide too slowly because you don't recognise that a quick decision is needed, you risk losing clients, market share, money or team members. Putting off decisions through fears of getting it wrong, or not wanting to deal with the consequences of a decision you know will be unpopular, can be costly.

A fast-changing hybrid space with no physical edges can make the capture of relevant data feel like chasing dandelion wisps floating through the air. The priority is to design information flows in your organisation and with your team that ensure you (and key decision-makers) receive what you need when you need it, and leakages of important data are minimised.

The drive to get to the destination as fast as possible, especially if you have shareholders demanding explanations, can derail wisdom. In a turbulent world, the direction of travel becomes increasingly important. Mode of travel is important too. It isn't only about where you are going. It's about how you are moving on your way there; how you are affecting yourself and others in the organisation and beyond with your choices. Whatever the situation, a key question to ask is: 'Who has been affected by this decision and what has that impact been?'

Cultivating a new relationship with decisions

As our world gets more complex, the decisions you and your team face mirror that complexity. 'Wicked problems' is a term coined by urban planners to describe problems that cannot be solved by traditional linear approaches, do not have one 'right' answer and involve many interdependent stakeholders with differing values. Decisions of this nature in the workplace invite you into a new relationship with decision-making that is curious, open-minded and alert.

Being curious involves a willingness to take action to experiment and discover impact. When there are no precedents and a high level of interdependency, creating mini experiments to support your decision-making helps you test out the consequences of actions before any great investment, allows you to learn incrementally and minimises the feeling of unacceptable risk.

'Fox thinking' can help you stay open-minded to solutions. In *The Neo Generalist*, Kenneth Mikkelsen and Richard Martin highlight the differences between hedgehog thinking and fox thinking.[26] Hedgehog thinking depends on what is known and is more closed. With a single-minded pursuit of one right answer, you might miss an unexpected solution presenting itself. By contrast, fox thinking, with its ease in times of ambiguity and ability to blend conflicting ideas, supports you to engage in decision-making in a way that allows you to arrive at unexpected, enlightening solutions.

Alertness to what is happening now is key throughout the whole process because we can't take for granted that our assumptions are correct or that, once made, our decisions will turn out as planned, or stay relevant for long in constantly evolving markets, customer and employee needs.

Evaluating decisions

Evaluation helps you stay alert post-decision. You will have your own ways of evaluating decisions based on the type and purpose of the decision, as well as the approach to decision cycles that you adopt in your business.

For the Stability Effect, what's important is that you have clarity about how you are defining good and bad outcomes and about who is judging this. From one vantage point, if a decision is made in alignment with what your organisation stands for, it can only be a bad decision when it isn't managed and implemented well and there's been poor communication around it.

Evaluation becomes a key learning opportunity when you bring curiosity and humility to the process. Curiosity helps you ask different questions and let go of assumptions. Humility helps you stay open to what's emerging, even if that outcome involves twists, turns and surprises. This can be hard for aspects of the ego, and we can block learning with fixed pre-conceived ideas about what 'should' happen and an 'I know best' attitude. We can't control everything, and we don't know all the answers.

Gaining awareness about decision-making in your team

Some decisions are yours to make. Others are for your team members to make. Some are for you and your team to make together through a collaborative process. It's important to understand the current quality of decision-making, both individually and collectively in your team, and identify what needs to change. Come together and explore your decision-making strengths and weaknesses as a team. Is there a need to work towards new decision-making attitudes?

While a team must present a united front, the reality is you are all individuals too. In any team, there are differing personalities at play. All key decision-makers will do well to understand their decision-making style. To make the best decisions and minimise the dangers of groupthink, a healthy business environment allows both individuality and a unified identity.

To gain more awareness about decision-making in your team, ask yourself:

- How do you decide who decides what?
- What is the quality of the team's decision-making in a changing world?
- Do you give your team full autonomy? How are they handling this?
- To what extent does what you stand for as a business guide decision-making in your team?
- What processes do you use for decision-making?

CASE STUDY:
Robert and his team are struggling to keep up

Robert heads up the corporate finance division of a large organisation. The theme for a recent away day with his senior team was decision-making in the post-pandemic world. The morning focused on current practices. What quickly became clear was an inconsistency of approach among people and insufficient time dedicated to updating decision-making processes to make them relevant in the new world of work.

Key information was not being shared, people weren't paying attention to what was going on in the environment around them and there was no consensus on what was important or who needed to know what. The whole team had been in the office together only once in the last two weeks. This was not unusual, and their sense of belonging was suffering. Two key projects were off-track and there was confusion about why, and how to improve the situation.

Robert tried to listen openly as each person spoke about decision-making in their business areas, but he found himself getting impatient. When the COO said he hadn't yet made a key decision that Robert had assumed was sorted and implemented, Robert nearly blew a fuse. Everyone noticed. Psychological safety in the team was low and accountability high. The result was anxiety.[27]

The key action from the morning was a commitment to get together in person for an hour at 10am every Monday and hold a Team Learning Lab meeting with 'decisions update' as a recurring agenda item.

For the afternoon session of the away day, Robert had invited a consultant to present on how to read the environment, a subject he was keen to learn more about and get the team trained on. We'll meet Robert and his team again at the end of Chapter 4 to find out how the afternoon went.

CHAPTER EXERCISE: You and your changing landscape

To embed the learnings of this chapter and apply them to your situation, ask yourself:

- What three words describe your attitude towards reflective practice?
- What three words describe how you relate to your team when they are learning?

- What three words describe how you and your team make decisions in the changing workplace landscape?

Summary

To thrive in a changing workplace landscape, you and your team need to change too. As you step onto the second part of your IRON pathway to stability in your organisation, you must:

- Understand that leadership has changed and is changing

- Recognise reading the environment as a crucial new leadership skill

- Cultivate real learning in your business

- Prioritise a sense of belonging in your team

- Spotlight how you and your team currently make decisions

FOUR
Deeper Listening

'It is the disease of not listening, the malady of not marking, that I am troubled withal.'
—William Shakespeare[28]

My cat seeks me out for company when a storm is coming. Cows sit down when it's going to rain. Dogs behave strangely before thunder starts to roll. Experts believe animals are acutely perceptive of minute changes in the environment. With their super senses, they pick up shifts in barometric pressure and humidity. They can hear, feel and smell environmental changes that people ordinarily do not, and then respond swiftly.[29]

While we typically do not notice subtle transitions in our environment, the profound changes in our workplace demand an extraordinary level of observation and the development of new skills. People can and do have the capacity to draw on human super senses to read their environment. It's simply a case of paying attention in a new way.

Take firefighters as an example. A firefighter in Illinois ordered his team to get out of a burning building during attempts to put a fire out. Moments later, the floor they had been standing on collapsed. A researcher who studied decision-making spoke to the firefighter afterwards. He discovered that he had noticed three unusual things: the fire was unusually quiet, the room was unusually hot and water was not putting out the fire as it usually would. A part of the firefighter's brain, beyond his awareness, knew that the fire was also in the basement, making the fire so quiet and the room they were standing in so hot. He had read the environment swiftly and knew the situation was not safe.[30]

We can read the environment for signs of good news, too. A female leader coming to the end of a career break to raise three children told me she knew an informal meeting to discuss a possible role was going to be life-changing. She trusted herself, secured childcare, took this casual chat seriously and gave it all she had. She was in a new role within a month, and it did change her life.

The firefighter, the returning-to-work mum, the cat, the cows and the dogs are all examples of people and animals reading the environment that they are in and taking action to move away from threats or towards opportunities.

In this chapter, we explore how you can read your environment, starting with your team, as those closest to you. However, the principles we discuss can also be applied to the wider environment in the business: your clients, customers, suppliers, shareholders and, beyond that, your local and regional markets and communities, your country etc. When you know how to read the environment and model it for your team, they learn how to do it and can pass this important skill on so that it spreads out into your organisation.

What is deeper listening?

Deeper listening is a term I use to describe the quality of attention needed for leaders to read the environment. It is only available when you are steady inside and it draws on *all* your senses – because you can and do listen with more than just your ears.

Ask someone with impaired hearing how they listen and they might say they do it with their eyes (by lip reading or watching sign language), with their nose (picking up the differing scents around them), with their body (sensing the feel of a place, its temperature and atmosphere), with their heart (sensitivity to love and fear) and with their head (common sense and deeper wisdom).

However many of these faculties are available to you, chances are, you aren't using them to best effect. Right now, you need them more than ever. There are a multitude of compelling (and unconvincing), noisy (and quiet), contradictory (and confirming) voices in the room (and in the media) seeking your attention. Add in the explosion of virtual reality, and knowing who to listen to has become a huge problem.

When you do listen deeply, you gain a discerning receptivity to your outer and inner environments and can engage in a keener level of noticing and learning than is otherwise possible. You can listen beyond outer noise and your inner noise, to a truth within where accurate perception lives. You won't be easily fooled and can sniff out trustworthy sources of information. This can safeguard you from low-level manipulation right up to being completely taken in by untruths and fake news. You can make better decisions for yourself and the business, build trust in your own judgement and your team and key stakeholders will trust you more.

Deeper listening involves listening to what's being said and what's not being said, aligning the intelligences of your head, heart and gut/body and recognising reality. It requires you to stay open and listen to both yourself and others, even when it gets uncomfortable. This is a risky business because you hear things beyond your own pre-conceptions. You might hear something that you didn't want to hear and, once heard, cannot be unheard. You might encounter difficult and uncomfortable truths. What others (and the deeper, wiser you) are communicating to you may change your perspective. The extent to which you are changed is your choice but the active engagement with what you have heard opens you up to growth and evolution.

While most of us don't engage in deeper listening in our day-to-day, it is a learnable skill. What's key is noticing your listening tendencies, breaking unhelpful patterns with intentional listening and discerning truth with my 'Listen Out, Listen In' process.

Noticing your listening tendencies

Most of us listen habitually, unconsciously hearing what we always hear, whether inwardly or outwardly. The critics hear what's wrong; the reason they/we/it aren't/isn't good enough. The people pleasers hear a way to impress and make someone happy. The empathetic ones hear the upset, the anger and the emotional human experience. The ambivalent hear mixed messages, a confusion, a reason to do nothing.

We listen unconsciously, utilising our filters. Filters arise because of our upbringing, life experience, education and professional training. They are necessary and help us do our jobs and live without being overwhelmed. They become a problem when they are so habitual that we lose the flexibility to discern what's really going on.

Think about your listening habits. Who do you find easy to listen to? Who do you find hard to listen to? Which member of your team can change your mind? Whose opinion do you dismiss? Perhaps you gravitate to the loudest and most confident-sounding voice around the table. Maybe you disconnect from the person who needs encouragement to speak up or the one with different views to you.

Why you listen relates to your underlying motivation. Habitually, you might listen for mistakes, barriers, possibilities, inconsistencies and why something might or might not work. All these are useful – until they're not. When they become rigid ways to meet your environment, you've lost the capacity to discern. You can delude yourself about your why. You might think you are listening to discover something new, to find a way forward or to evaluate options. However, when you dig deeper into your motives, you could find you are listening to prove yourself right, to feel good or to justify a previous decision.

Deeper listening becomes possible as you become more self-aware. So much of the who and why of your listening can slip under your radar. Self-awareness saves you from wasted time and energy and, importantly, gets you to better choices faster. The better you know yourself, your listening habits and your leanings towards excessive optimism or pessimism, your tendency to get dragged into distractions or lose yourself in entanglements, the better able you will be to discern the truth of information. The truth-teller within you learns to recognise the quality of truth and trust it.

Ultimately, the threads you follow in your listening depend on what you consider leadership to be.

DAILY PRACTICE: Noticing my listening tendencies

A useful way to begin moving towards deeper listening is to practise noticing your habitual tendencies in relation to who you listen to and why you listen. Take a few minutes at the end of each day to make a note of the who and the why of your listening that day. Review your notes at the end of each week. What insights do you have about your listening tendencies? What's helpful/unhelpful? What are you learning?

Break unhelpful habits with intentional listening

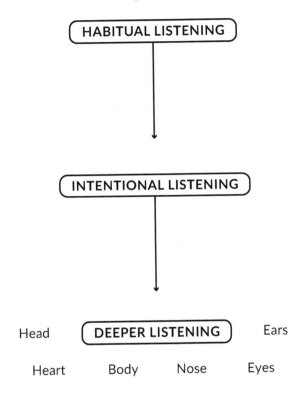

As shown in the diagram above, intentional listening is the developmental bridge between habitual listening and deeper listening. It provides a deliberate focus for your listening and, over time, releases unhelpful ingrained ways of listening. If you adopt an intentional listening practice like the one below, this will support your progress.

WEEKLY PRACTICE: Intentional listening

Choose one day each week to be fully intentional about who you listen to and why you listen. In real-time, on-the-job situations set intentions as follows:

- Who: intend to listen to people you don't usually listen to. Make a list of these people to keep yourself accountable.

- Why: intend to listen with motivations that are different to the unhelpful habitual ones you've identified. Make a list of your intentional motivations – for example, listening for peoples' strengths rather than weaknesses.

At the end of the day, take a few minutes to make notes on the learnings and insights gleaned from your intentional listening. Reflect on the effect intentional listening has had on you, your team, your leadership and your decisions that day.

Done regularly, intentional listening can reveal new and valuable information for you to feed into your leadership and decision-making processes. You can see it in action over a full working week in the case study at the end of the chapter.

The 'Listen Out, Listen In' process

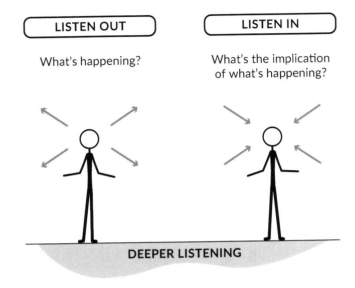

LISTEN OUT

What's happening?

LISTEN IN

What's the implication
of what's happening?

DEEPER LISTENING

My 'Listen Out, Listen In' process guides you to discern truth in the world outside and inside you. It is based on deeper listening and leads you to the realm of accurate perception that lives beyond your habitual filters. The process involves taking seriously your own deeper guidance system of feelings, thoughts and bodily sensations.

Listen out

'Listen out' is outward-focused. You notice what's happening around you with your team, what's being said and not said, the atmosphere in the room, what you see and don't see in their presence. Listening out is an in-the-moment activity, although there may be something you remember later that you didn't pick up on at the time.

The minute you're promoted into a position of leadership, staying in touch with what's going on around you gets harder. Listening out becomes critical. Hybrid working adds a new dimension to listening out because you're not necessarily physically in a room with people. The following practices will support you in listening out.

DAILY PRACTICE: What's happening?

At intervals in your day, look up from what you're doing and pay attention to what's happening around you. You can set alarms on your phone to remind you to do this. Whether you're working from home or in the office, take a metaphorical step back and notice with curiosity what is happening in that moment. Connect to your breath as a primary means of relating to your surroundings, to steady you inside and take you into deeper listening. What's unusual, surprising or ordinary? Make a note of your responses in your phone or a journal. Review your notes at the end of each week.

DAILY PRACTICE: Virtual listening out

Practise listening out in your interactions with your team on Zoom, MS Teams or whichever virtual platforms you use. Pay attention to body

---

language, tone and pace of voice and what people say and don't say. Make a note of the things you notice about individual team members, or the team collectively, that had an impact on you. Review your notes at the end of each week. The aim is to become as observant through a screen as you are in person (or more so).

Listen in

'Listen in' is inward-focused. You notice what's happening inside of you and seek the guidance of your deeper thoughts, feelings and bodily sensations in relation to what you notice 'out there' that has an impact on you. The aim of listening in is to reach an understanding or 'knowingness' about a situation, meeting, project, encounter or conversation. It takes you beyond habitual ways of perceiving to accurately interpret and assess the implication of what you noticed 'out there' and becomes a platform for action.

Listening in can occur in the moment or through reflection. For most of us, reflection is necessary for two reasons. First, real life usually reveals truth gradually and we need to stay connected to it as it's unfolding. Second, we are not able to accurately discern in the moment. This is not because of our inadequacy, but because of the strength of our filters.

Take a team meeting situation where you notice something is 'off' in the way people are speaking to each other. Imagine you have a full agenda and a deadline to meet. You might be tempted to dismiss what you've noticed or wade in with an interpretation based on your filters with their unexamined thinking and reactions. You might also go into automatic problem-solving mode, to analyse, work things out and reach an immediate conclusion.

A listening-in approach involves taking a few minutes at the end of the day to pay attention to your deeper thoughts, feelings and sensations in relation to what you noticed to reach the truest and most accurate interpretation of what's going on, and the implications of this. Most likely, this will not happen straight away. Rather, you will continue to pay attention to team dynamics the next day, and the day after. You will notice and learn more. Through continued listening in, new insights, awareness and understandings – all the things that help you read the environment accurately – can surface. Answers that come from this place have a different quality and, over time and with practice, you will begin to recognise it.

The 'off-ness' that your problem-solving mind might have attributed to things that have happened in the past, like unresolved disputes between two team members whose personalities clash, could be pointing to a deeper concern that several members of your team are feeling, without any of them consciously knowing what is going on. This latter interpretation could lead you to decide to sensitively explore with the team what concerns they are holding onto and discover critical new information relating to an important project.

When you listen in, over time you develop the wisdom to allow the problems, challenges and opportunities to just be until further information arises from within you or the outside world and reveals a way forward. You might test your understanding and fine-tune your perception of what's going on until you know what to do. Things that were questions and places of uncertainty become clear, and not because you've worked them out with your surface-level thinking. The questions have been in a holding place, and clarity has come through deeper listening. In circumstances like these, it is slow, considered action that shows leadership.

Listening in can also be an in-the-moment or urgent activity. At the extreme, it's lifesaving and instinctive – like the firefighter in Illinois. You know what must be done and you do it. In these circumstances, it is swift, confident action that shows leadership.

Below is a simple practice that combines listening out and listening in for one-to-one situations, to help you read the environment of your team.

> **WEEKLY PRACTICE: Checking in with my team**
>
> Check in with each team member consistently, and at least weekly, to counter the risk brought by the variability of hybrid work that some people slip through the net of your awareness. Ask people how they are, what's worrying them, what's bringing them joy and what they're noticing.
>
> Listen out to what they say in an expanded way, not just with your ears, but with all your senses, and with your body and heart as well as your mind. Listen to what's not being said. Listen to your inner guidance for the truest and most reliable interpretation of what people are telling you and consider its implications.

A desire to respond with integrity

The 'Listen Out, Listen In' process, whether gradual and conscious over time or fast and immediate, brings you to choice and action. We need leaders who want to and do choose and act with integrity. This motivation generates the highest quality of listening and behaviour. Without it, leadership can overtly or secretly become an ego trip or a place where you lose yourself and your soul. If this sounds dramatic, think for a moment about corporate corruption and company downfalls. Behind most disaster scenarios is a leader who has lost their integrity.

Responding with integrity means acting honestly and with a moral compass. It also means acting from the integrated intelligence that can be accessed through deeper listening. With integrity, you cannot be persuaded into positions that undermine what you stand for. There could be times when your inner guidance goes against the majority voice. If that's what's needed, responding with integrity means trusting that voice. In the words of Carly Fiorina, when she was CEO of Hewlett-Packard: 'To build a great company, which is a CEO's job, sometimes you have to stand up against conventional wisdom.'[31]

If you're ever in doubt about how to respond to a situation, think about the consequences. What's your sense of where your anticipated course of action leads? What's the likely effect on the people around you, the planet and the bottom line? Is there an overall transmission of life outwards, in the way that the element of iron enables oxygen to reach all parts of the body?

People will notice you responding with integrity. When you model it, they will follow. You become a catalyst for others to respond with integrity too. With that as the standard, reading the environment and discerning what's needed for the greater good becomes the new norm.

CASE STUDY: An intentional listening week begins training the team to read the environment

Let's return to Robert and his team on their away day. The afternoon presentation on reading the environment had a big impact. Robert wanted to get into listening out and listening in straight away, but he realised that practising intentional listening was a necessary first step to loosen the grip of habitual thinking. He and the team agreed on an Intentional Listening Week with a primary focus on interactions between each other and a secondary focus on interactions with everyone encountered during the working day.

On Monday, the team (including Robert) set an intention to listen for strengths. On Tuesday, the intention was to listen for inefficiencies. On Wednesday, it was listening for engagement. Thursday was listening for innovation, and Friday was listening for the quality of relationships. They made brief notes each day to capture their experiences.

At 4pm on Friday, the team gathered online to discuss what they had learned. Initially, it had been hard to listen in a way that wasn't habitual for them. They'd all felt self-conscious, but by midweek people were enjoying the focus on listening. Interactions with each other seemed richer and they were learning things they didn't know.

That week, listening for strengths and connections revealed valuable new information. On two occasions, different team members had noticed that Paul, the new head of private equity, was skilled at spotting conflict arising and defusing fraught situations.

It turned out that Paul was a brown belt in jujitsu. Being centred, deeper listening and reading situations were second nature to him. Paul hadn't made the connection between his years of training on centring outside of work and reading the environment in a work context. He did it instinctively and in the moment. Everyone in the team now wanted to know how. Paul had a wealth of bodily and spatial awareness experience that he agreed to share to build on the mind-based focus of the consultant's presentation and enhance the team's deeper listening.

At the end of their meeting, the team agreed to continue the practice of intentional listening into the next week, this time tailored to their work priorities, and to pair up for two minutes daily for accountability check-ins.

CHAPTER EXERCISE: Just 10 minutes, Part Two

Sit (or walk) for just 10 minutes at the end of each day, for three consecutive days, and reflect on:

- Three things that you have heard, felt, seen or noticed today in your team or organisation that have had an impact on you
- The potential implications of these three things
- Three actions your wisest self invites you to take tomorrow in response to these three things (one for each thing)

You can make this exercise a practice by doing it on an ongoing basis.

Summary

Reading the environment in turbulent conditions requires deeper listening. This involves:

- Listening inclusively with all your senses, your body, heart and head
- Knowing your listening tendencies
- Breaking unhelpful patterns with intentional listening
- Listening out (noticing what's happening 'out there') and listening in (accurately interpreting and discerning the implications of what you've noticed)
- A desire to respond with integrity

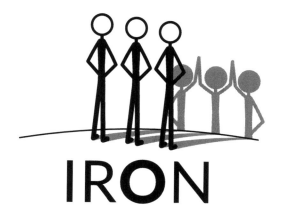

IRON

PART THREE
OVERCOMING CHALLENGES

N ow you're primed for inner steadiness and have insight into how you can read your environment, it's time to focus on what might get in the way of these, and of you, your team and your organisation realising the potential and possibilities of this unique era. In times of ongoing change, the fear factor is stronger than in more stable times and challenges can derail, fracture and disconnect people. How you handle difficulties makes all the difference. Draw on qualities of the element of iron, like resilience and the capacity to unite with others, to stand you in good stead as you steer your organisation through stormy waters towards the results you want. Sometimes you can overcome challenges swiftly and completely; other times, you need to live and lead alongside them, without being controlled by them.

Whatever scenario you face, the path forward involves being aware of challenges and discovering ways to move beyond them. This is the work of the two chapters in Part Three. Chapter 5 identifies potential challenges, and Chapter 6 focuses on how to move beyond them. It's important work because dealing with challenges is how you evolve and grow, individually and collectively. Challenges are the gateway to transformation.

FIVE

What Is It That Is Holding You Back?

'If you can find a path with no obstacles,
it probably doesn't lead anywhere.'
—Frank A Clark[32]

History is filled with breakthroughs, of the impossible made possible. New realities emerge
that shift the trajectory of humankind. When these
moments arise, some people take the lead and clear
the way of obstacles, so others can follow. These are
the pathfinders who have within them the motivation,
courage and persistence to acknowledge and overcome challenges to become the pioneers of the future.

If you're reading this book, the chances are you are
a pathfinder in the business world. The call to lead

in transitional times is a stretching one. When you recognise that what we are talking about here is an emergent journey of leadership and organisational transformation, you appreciate why. Inward fears and outer obstacles can hold you back. Acknowledging and being ready for these is key to moving beyond them.

In this chapter, we will identify some of the challenges that you and your team can encounter in changing times. In the personal sphere, these might be navigating uncertainty, thinking traps and leadership tensions. For you and your team, relationship issues and alignment challenges can increase in intensity in times of change and present difficulties. Old systems and processes and the distracted world we live in can also be a barrier for you in your leadership.

These challenges are not an exhaustive list. The topics we cover are designed to get you thinking about your own context, because with awareness comes choice.

Navigating uncertainty

A masterclass participant once asked me 'How do I conquer uncertainty?' Speaking for many, her question revealed an ingrained battle mindset where there must be a winner and a loser. Given that investors were reviewing their future involvement in the business, and she was personally going through a divorce, you can understand why she wanted to put uncertainty in an armlock, wrestle it to the ground for answers and conquer it once and for all.

My reply of 'You don't' was a bitter pill for her to swallow. Former leadership training had placed importance on certainty and outcomes, and her current success was largely a result of her ability to control her environment and know the answers. The things that had helped her excel and been enablers in her career in a more stable world were now holding her back. She was being asked to fundamentally change her relationship to uncertainty and the unknown.

Uncertainty is an inherent, unavoidable aspect of both wanted and unwanted change. It is associated with a state of not knowing. Right now, you might not know what's going to happen, who to be, what to think, what to do or who to trust. It's understandable that many in positions of leadership, with the responsibility that involves, fear the unknown. Think about your upbringing and education. In the West, we were raised in societies that value knowing the answer, getting it right and being in control. These values are ingrained in our belief systems and drive our needs, but they are notoriously difficult to uphold in the unknown, unpredictable and risky terrain of uncertainty.

In his article 'Why we're hard-wired to hate uncertainty', Marc Lewis describes a study by scientist Archy de Berker and colleagues that showed that uncertainty is more stressful than knowing that something bad is definitely going to happen.[33] This is why waiting to hear whether a key investor wants to continue with you or not, or whether a major staff issue is resolved or will hit the national papers, is more disturbing than hearing the worst-case news. At least then you know where you stand.

Neuroscience helps us understand this illogical reality. Over millions of years of evolution, the reward centre of the brain, the striatum, has developed the capacity to anticipate good and bad consequences. It even predicts the odds of these consequences and becomes highly aroused as those odds approach the peak of uncertainty at 50% when things could go either way. At this point, most of us feel extremely stressed and our brain chemistry is on high threat alert. On top of this, when faced with uncertainty, the mind often tricks us into thinking the worst. We imagine a variety of bad outcomes coming our way and overestimate their effect and duration.[34]

It's no wonder, then, that the uncertainty that you, your team and your wider workforce are experiencing as your organisation transitions from old to new ways of working and being in business has the potential to derail you.

Traps and tensions

Thinking traps and leadership tensions are part of humanity but, left untended, they hinder progress towards the leader you are becoming and your key business goals. They may have remained hidden in the more stable world of the past. Now, in an uncertain world with nervous systems on high alert, they surface. Do you know what your tendencies are, and where they lead you? Let's have a look at some of the traps you might fall into.

Traps

In our context, I define thinking traps as erroneous thoughts about change, decision-making and ourselves. Thinking traps show up in our attachments to the old and our inability to move forward. They send us into a state of anxiety, which we sometimes bury and are not consciously aware of. Thinking traps invariably make change, decision-making and leadership a challenge.

A common trap related to change is getting stuck in the status quo. As the name suggests, status quo thinking tricks us into working hard to repeat the past and keep things the same. We might imagine this gives us stability, and in the short term it can, but as a repeated habit of mind, all it leads to is stagnation. We don't listen in and act on what we hear from our inner guidance because we fear the change and growth this demands. It's almost impossible to repeat the past in current circumstances, so falling into the status quo trap when you're in a leadership position generates inner turmoil associated with fighting change, avoiding the big decisions and repeating past choices that no longer fit current circumstances. You might hire people unsuited to a role but who are similar to predecessors or yourself, choose services from outdated suppliers you are familiar with or stay in declining markets that you know well. In the status quo, there is comfort in the known, which is why you get trapped there.

As well as the status quo trap, there are other traps that can hold you back:[35]

- The **sunk cost** trap sees you staying in something because of the time, energy and money you've already invested, irrespective of whether it's a match for you now. That 'something' could be a business strategy, an organisational structure, an office building, a home, a relationship, a career.

- The **confirming evidence** trap persuades you to seek out information that supports your existing viewpoint and maintains you as 'right'.

- The **'just do it'** trap goads you into taking action before the time is right.

- The **Achilles heel** trap works on your weak spot. It makes you acquiesce to an aspect of your personality that leads you astray. This might be the part of you that has to say yes to things that offer flattery or glamour and subsequently pursue a course of action that isn't the best route.

- The trap of **unhealthy perfectionism** sees you waiting for the perfect set of circumstances before you act. It keeps you fine-tuning your ideas, your strategy papers and your brilliance, as the moment for action passes you by. You can also get trapped in your beliefs about yourself, what you can and can't do and what's possible and not possible.

There are many more traps: the 'no time to think' trap; unconscious people pleasing or approval seeking; unconscious bias predicting what and who people are, based on a set of characteristics; comparing yourself to others; being self-critical and unforgiving towards yourself.

I've seen self-criticism in particular block high-achieving clients from reading the environment, for example. When fast-paced high achievers slow down enough to touch their inner guidance about what's happening in their team, business or life, their perception that they are not reaching their own high standards can storm in and sabotage any useful action. This can become a chicken and egg situation. There's a reluctance to slow down, notice and listen in because self-criticism kicks in and that feels bad. However, when you don't listen, there's no possibility to learn and do something different, and that feels bad too.

Knowing the thinking traps you are prone to is a key first step in moving beyond them. Whatever the trap, the result is the same. You get stuck, lose time, make poor choices and don't achieve important goals. All of this comes at an emotional and financial cost. Freeing yourself from traps, or at least loosening their grip, is critical to life and business if you are aiming to realise potential.

Tensions

Moving now to leadership tensions, these arise when values and priorities seem to pull in opposite directions: stick to the plan, adjust the plan; invest in team building, keep costs down; you decide, we decide; stay in your role, move on to a new challenge; rely on data, trust your gut; act now, wait for more information; in the office, out of the office.

Today's complex environment is bursting at the seams with tensions. They can occur within you as a person, between you and team members, among team members and organisationally between different departments. Some tensions have no near-term resolution and attempting to make a binary decision before the situation has ripened causes undue stress in already stress-provoking situations. Others are closer to a conclusion, and without skilful handling can block you from making decisions and acting. Tensions in the outer world are often mirrored in your inner world (and vice versa). You can feel conflicted and upset inside, and easily slip into polarised, black-and-white thinking to cope with the discomfort.

A significant tension all of us need to handle in an era of transformation is the liminal space between one world ending and the new one beginning. When leaders lose their way in navigating this tension, so too does the organisation they lead. In this 'space in between' there will be necessary losses. A lack of clarity over what we need to let go of is a subtle but real barrier to moving forward and gaining momentum. If we don't understand what is ending, it is difficult to step fully into what is beginning. Instead, we stay in a fog of indecision and confusion for longer than is necessary. In my own life and business, challenges in acknowledging what is ending and letting go of it have led to transition periods lasting years instead of months. The associated cost can be high, whether physical, emotional, mental, spiritual, financial or a combination of all these.

What is ending could be personal: a belief you have about yourself, an attitude, an outlook on the world, a habit or an outdated way of leading or doing business. It could also be organisational: a strategy, a key product, a service or a client. In a similar vein, knowing what you are holding onto and taking with you into the future helps you gain the strength to get moving.

Spotting traps and tensions

While traps and tensions are different, inner upset tends to arise with both. This is a useful sign that something is holding you back that warrants your attention. You might be more reactive and less empathetic than usual, or feel nothing inside. Your body might be carrying extra physical tension with associated symptoms of headaches or low energy. I recently saw a new client crossing a station platform. His head was down and his upper body stooped over as if he was walking into a strong headwind. His posture told a story of traps and tensions, of carrying heavy burdens and pushing forward against persistent, wearying barriers. This would inevitably show up in his leadership.

Other signs that traps and tensions have a hold on you include denying that change is happening, secretly fighting your reality or saying no to something that matters to you. Fear underpins many traps, so naming your fears can help you quickly see where you are caught. Paradoxically, you might become intensely busy when traps and tensions have you in a hold, to avoid acknowledging what's going on for you. You might resist the solitude that would help you see and feel what's happening. You might go up a notch with unhelpful criticism. Guilt, shame and blame can elbow their way in.

All these inner movements can arise without traps and tensions being the root cause, but they can also be strong indicators that something is going on inside that is blocking you, and with the right kind of attention, it can be released or minimised.

Teamworking challenges

Navigating uncertainty, traps and tensions can also hold your team members back at a personal level. For teamwork, the extra pressure that change brings tends to magnify relationship and alignment issues, both of which negatively affect decision-making and stability in the business.

Weak relationships

Strong relationships are about trust and respect. Without these qualities, bad habits can creep in, weaken relationships and block the flow of information and intelligence between you and your team. Take gossip, for instance. Name-calling, back-stabbing and spreading rumours aren't just the territory of in-crowds, outsiders and scapegoats in high school. In organisations, team gossip can be devastating and create toxic, divided environments. In worst-case scenarios, gossip can result in dismissals and unfounded rumours can lead to unwanted resignations of talented people.

Another bad relationship habit that many teams suffer from is unresolved conflict. When you don't sort out issues promptly, you waste time, money and energy. A client told me that she replayed a contentious conversation with her colleague over and over in her mind for days after the event. She perceived there was an injustice and felt infuriated with the other person's behaviour. While there was an element of not knowing how to resolve things, a bigger part of her story was working in a team culture that didn't feel safe enough to have the real conversations needed to sort out conflict. Instead, it was brushed under the carpet, seen as a negative thing and left to fester and cause further damage down the line.

Teams that can't have real conversations struggle with resolving conflict and run the risk of vital information for learning and decision-making remaining hidden. It is worth reflecting on how safe people feel to be real with you and speak the truth. You might know you're open to hearing what's going on, but things get in the way of people speaking up. They might be holding onto events that have happened in the past. They might think the truth is career-limiting. You might be trapped in old ideas about them and unknowingly be transmitting a 'do not disturb' message that they can sense. Whatever the reasons for it, an absence of real conversations is a barrier to stability and good decisions. Even when there is trust and respect in teams, things can go wrong and hold you back. Being human is an imperfect occupation.

Lack of alignment

Stability and decision-making also suffer when your team (and you) have lost connection and alignment with what you stand for – most notably, the deeper purpose of the business and the vision of where you are going.

This can happen for obvious reasons like personal upsets that affect someone's motivation and sense of identity. Divorce, re-locating and bereavement are just some of the events of a human life that can adversely affect our capacity to engage with our work, see clearly and choose wisely. Business-related changes like new ownership can also have a huge impact on a team's alignment with its purpose and connection to what the business is about. A client shared with me the unrest she had observed since the business had been sold to a distant holding company. Day-to-day operations continued as before, but the invisible foundations of the business rested on a new source, people's sense of belonging was slipping away and the top team were losing motivation. They seemed uncaring, and they were dropping balls left right and centre.

The emergence of a hybrid workplace has, in some instances, put more strain on team relationships and alignment with what the business stands for. When these things weaken, you can find yourselves in a downward spiral of individualism and dissatisfaction. This can be hard to get out of unless you act quickly.

Outdated systems and processes

Systems and processes that worked in a more predictable world and haven't caught up with the current needs of hybrid business block progress. Like many organisations, you could be finding that the work you have done and are doing to redesign your workplace for hybrid working is flushing out old systems and process issues that have been there for years but haven't needed to be addressed as a priority until now.

Two such areas that influence leaders are recruitment and performance-management systems and processes. You know that the calibre of your team is critical for stability and delivering on goals and targets. Yet getting the right talent and perspectives then keeping hold of them and realising their potential can be a major challenge. Some things that get in the way include difficulties finding the right people in a tight market; inflexibility in the role requirements in a world that demands flexibility; not knowing what talent and development you need in a post-pandemic world; your industry being perceived as 'unsexy'; a poor organisation or team reputation; measuring and rewarding outcomes and behaviours that undermine the safety and trust you are seeking to build and don't align with your purpose and values.

Our distracted world

To close, we must acknowledge the challenge of living, leading and working in a chaotic, distracted world. Without awareness of this, you can slip into accepting constant external stimuli as normal and become incredibly distracted. This robs you of your inner steadiness and you become vulnerable to over-thinking, losing perspective and getting entangled in unhelpful emotional charge. If you ever find yourself feeling like a victim, rescuing people or bullying, chances are you're in relationship dynamics that don't serve you or others.

Constant 'doing' robs you of the space to take a sense check of what's going on around you and listen for important information that isn't immediately apparent. As you lose the ability to read the environment and make wise decisions, short-term needs are placed above long-term priorities. Together, this is a potent mix of challenges to stability.

CASE STUDY: Oliver is stuck

Oliver is the CEO of a medium-sized business. The pandemic accelerated the growth of the company and he feels out of his depth. With an impossibly busy schedule, he barely has time to think beyond what is needed in the moment. Oliver consistently holds onto his workload and doesn't trust his team with high-stakes clients or tasks. Morale is low. People don't talk to each other beyond functional task-related matters. Things haven't been the same since the CMO left for reasons Oliver still doesn't understand. The interim replacement isn't working. Oliver knows he needs to recruit someone new but hasn't been able to secure anyone who will work full-time and be office-based, two requirements he is sticking to even though it's not needed in the context. Oliver is putting off key decisions, both in the business and his personal life, because he doesn't have space to consider them properly. His children have recently left home and his marriage is entering a new phase. He doesn't know what the future holds and isn't sure what he wants. This makes him feel uneasy as he's always been clear on that in the past. Just before the pandemic, Oliver had persuaded key business stakeholders that it was the right time to invest in a new IT system. He is frustrated and embarrassed that it's already out of date and isn't meeting the new demands of a hybrid workforce. Oliver persistently struggles with neck and shoulder tension, and related headaches.

Oliver's situation suggests that the things that are holding him back include difficulties navigating uncertainty; the 'no time to think' and status quo traps; discomfort having open conversations with the team; and outdated recruitment expectations and systems. We'll meet Oliver again at the end of Chapter 6 to see how he moved beyond these barriers.

CHAPTER EXERCISE: What might hold you back?

To start making progress towards overcoming your blockers, consider:

• What three things are ending for you personally (beliefs, self-concept, attitude, outlook on the world etc) and what three things are beginning as you move into the new world of work?

• What three thinking traps are you most vulnerable to?

• What three leadership tensions are you currently dealing with?

Summary

Key factors that can hold you and your team back from building environments of dynamic stability, better decision-making and realised potential include:

• Difficulties navigating uncertainty

• Thinking traps and leadership tensions

• Relationship and alignment issues in your team

• Outdated systems and processes

• The distracted world we live in

SIX
Moving Beyond Challenges

'Just as nature takes every obstacle, every impediment, and works around it – turns it to its purposes, incorporates it into itself – so, too, a rational being can turn each setback into raw material and use it to achieve its goal.'
—Marcus Aurelius[36]

A skilful, focused sailor can steer a boat across a stormy ocean, moving fast in the direction of travel when there are openings and holding tight when conditions are treacherous. Similarly, a courageous mountaineer can find a path through rocky, inhospitable terrain and the fog of low clouds to reach the summit before descent. The sailor and the mountaineer show us that it's not about never having challenges; it's about how we deal with challenges.

In this chapter, we look at how to move beyond the challenges discussed in Chapter 5. Your toolkit will include shifting your perception to relax into uncertainty, mind-body freedom techniques to move you through traps and tensions, mobilising your team through the 3Cs model, redefining new success measures and continually reviewing progress.

Relaxing into uncertainty

Shifting your relationship with uncertainty, and with yourself in uncertain conditions, might be one of the hardest and most important skills for a modern-day leader to master in a context of ongoing change. The capacity to do this will set you apart from those who haven't yet learned how.

Attitudes of curiosity, discovery and adventure lay strong foundations to perceive uncertainty in a way that nourishes you. This makes all the difference to your experience and leads you to value uncertainty for the creativity, growth and fruitfulness it can bring if you can stay with it. Uncertainty is where possibility resides and potential is uncovered. It is often in uncertainty that you ask the deeper questions that result in a breakthrough.

Quiet confidence comes with the understanding that uncertainty within or outside of you is a malleable space. Just as iron seems hard and invincible yet melts at a high temperature, uncertainty, though it seems inherently unknowable, can yield to your shaping of it. When you're able to resist premature urges to control and impose your will on uncertain situations and work alongside that uncertainty, new and innovative solutions can emerge.

Traditional motivational 'make it happen' attitudes don't belong in uncertainty. Instead, every time you shift out of worry, anxiety and fear into the responsiveness of inner steadiness, trust and openness, you take a step towards meeting the unknown as a worthy equal. This shift arises when you recruit your body, breath and nervous system to soften the tension that wants to lock into your experience and reframe uncertainty by asking:

- What's the opportunity in this uncertainty?

- What's the worst thing that can happen? What's the best?

- When has uncertainty led to positive results for me?

- What can I be certain about within this uncertain situation?

- I wonder what would happen if...?

Feeling completely at ease in uncertainty can be a lifelong process, especially for a leader carrying a lot of responsibility, with much at stake. When you've really had enough of uncertainty and long for the old days when things were more predictable, turn to the words of Winston Churchill for courage: 'Without this measureless and perpetual uncertainty, the drama of human life would be destroyed.'[37]

In other words, what would life be like with total, measurable certainty?

Mind-body freedom techniques

Let us turn now again to traps. While these are thinking errors, they are often part of a mind-body system that has an emotional and physical component. This means that as well as working with your thoughts to liberate yourself and get unstuck, you can work with your feelings and body.

Some traps are easy to shift, and awareness alone can do it. Others demand more conscious effort to release you from them. There are a few ways you can approach this.

Reappraisal

Thinking-based techniques for release include challenging your appraisal of a situation where the trap is operating. You can do this by:

- Viewing the situation from different perspectives: how would someone you admire see it? How would you at your best perceive it?

- Recalling times when you were free of the trap

- Being honest about your motivation. What does the trap give you and what's the payoff of being caught in it?

- Considering where the trap leads, if you don't escape it

- Reminding yourself of your goal

Address fear

If you want to go for the transformational jugular, address the (usually well-hidden) fear underpinning a trap. Take the 'confirming evidence' trap, for example. At its root is often a fear of being wrong or admitting you are wrong. Attached to this are your judgements about what this might result in and/or mean about you. Concerns about being ridiculed, feeling shamed or looking foolish can all nip away at your ankles and prevent you from moving forward.

Naming and accepting your fears can dissolve these concerns. You don't have to share your fears with anyone else, although that can be helpful (and healing) if you choose the right person. What's key is that you share them with yourself. We all have fears, however courageous we are. What gives them power over us is secrecy and denial. Freeing yourself from fear helps you reconnect with self-trust and inner strength; from that vantage point, you can see the new possibilities beyond the trap.

DAILY PRACTICE: Addressing fear

At the start or end of the day, get settled inside and ask yourself 'What am/was I afraid of today?' Say your response out loud, or write it down. Sometimes saying or writing down 'I'm afraid of being wrong', for instance, is enough to dissolve the fear. Other times, you need to feel and release the range of emotions tangled up with the fear, and proactively shift your perception to, for example, a thought like 'Discovering what's true is more important than being right.'

Body and energy work

When your mind can't find freedom from a trap on its own, involve your body and energy. The physical aspect of a trap is often felt in localised body tension. You can release this on your own through body stretching, breathwork and movement practices. For the longer-held, deeper areas of stuck-ness that have permeated cells and connective tissue, seeing a specialist can be beneficial. Deep tissue massage, craniosacral therapy or acupuncture sessions are some of the things you can try to release old tension in your body.

Body and energy work are closely linked. Some body work reconfigures the energy flows in your body; this shifts long-held emotions, thoughts and movement patterns and the influence they have. Similarly, some energy work shifts the body, emotions, thoughts and movement. The Emotional Freedom Technique (known as EFT, or tapping) is a scientifically proven energy tool to clear stuck patterns,[38] as is Reiki.[39]

WEEKLY PRACTICE: Body and energy sessions

When you are leading through fast change, body and energy work becomes a necessity, not a luxury. Find a modality that works for you and diarise weekly sessions with a trusted practitioner. Don't be a passive client. Getting involved in sessions makes them a practice. At the start of a session, set an intention, such as 'release' or 'clarity', to involve your mind. Feel your body as the session progresses. Monitor the impact.

Flexible thinking for leadership tensions

Just as it is for traps, awareness is important for overcoming leadership tensions. Without it, tensions can tear you apart. Expecting them to arise, within you and between you and your team, eases their resolution and permits for trade-offs to be made. To move through tensions, cultivate flexible thinking so that you can tolerate the ambiguity of multiple perspectives. Both/and thinking (rather than either/or) will help you counter the tendency to polarise, and it enables you to hold and balance opposing forces.

Take the tension between deciding now about investing in a new market versus waiting, watching and gathering more information. Accepting this tension as normal in fast-changing times will immediately shift your relationship to the decision and yourself making the decision, and reduces the chances that you'll get stuck in a rigid position.

You could find yourself simultaneously wanting to do different things. Often, I hear clients say 'a part of me wants to do X and another part wants to do Y.' With both/and thinking you can stay open and curious, avoid clinging to one position or another and move through the tension until you gain more insight.

Be curious. Can you look at your decision in new ways? Can you break it down into a chain of smaller decisions that still make steps towards your goal? Can you decide about part of it, and continue gathering data on the rest? Curiosity guides you to explore previously unseen options and keep taking purposeful, informed action through tension.

Self-compassion

Holding a compassionate stance towards yourself as you engage in challenges is another practice that supports your progress. Dr Kristin Neff defines self-compassion as an emotionally positive self-attitude that should protect against the negative consequences of self-judgement, isolation and rumination.[40] Compassion lies beyond the fear that triggers the nervous system. With it, you can accept where you (and others) are and turn away from inner conversations that aren't serving you. With an ongoing practice of self-compassion, it is possible to change the voice of your inner judge into one of empathy and understanding, to support you to meet difficulties in a courageous, helpful way.

DAILY PRACTICE: The voice of self-compassion

Whatever challenge or difficulty you're facing, notice your self-talk. Initially, it may be hard to do this in the moment, so set alarms on your phone for 10am, 1pm and 4pm to check in with how you're talking to yourself. When your self-talk disempowers you and unjustly gives you a hard time, learn to forgive yourself and find a way to bring the voice of compassion into the situation.

Experiment with more affirming, positive, encouraging self-talk about who you are and what you're capable of, noticing if you can how different expressions feel in your body. Imagine how a kind, caring friend might interpret what's happening and what they would say to you.

The aim is to find a self-compassionate voice that resonates with who you are and doesn't let you get lost in endless unhelpful self-analysis. It should support you and allow you to see clearly and

---

truthfully to enable you to make wise choices and take necessary actions. This can take time if your self-talk has become habitually harsh. It's worth it, though. Changing how you speak to yourself changes your brain chemistry and your emotional state, leaving you more resourceful.[41] Learning to rest in compassion doesn't preclude strength – it enhances it.

Mobilise your team with the 3Cs

Disruption in your team dynamics influences stability in your business. Whether it's the relationship and alignment challenges of Chapter 5, or issues unique to your team, my 3Cs Team Mobiliser model, with its pillars of Care, Communicate and Collaborate, can get your team working and moving together towards your goals. You and your team can apply the pillars to the specific blocks you want to overcome and check in with each other regularly to keep on track.

The 3Cs Team Mobiliser model

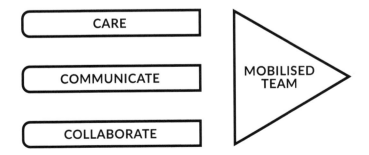

Care

The Care pillar prioritises relationships with work and each other. It is the realm of motivation and connection.

Do what it takes to get your team connected at the heart level with what the business is about. If this means taking a day out of your busy schedules to re-establish passion for and belief in the purpose, mission and vision of the business, do that. If it means going to meet the people who are positively influenced by what your business does, do that. When hearts are moved by seeing real people and situations transformed because of your business, the experience doesn't fade in a hurry. It's worth the time, energy and money to stay plugged into this. A heart that cares can move mountains.

Treat each other with respect and consideration. Take workload, for instance. Getting the balance right is an act of care. If you regularly work evenings and weekends while your team works Monday to Friday, 9 'til 5, the balance is off. The same is true of the reverse situation. If there is someone in your team (it might be you) who has experienced exhaustion and burnout in the last twelve months, the balance is off. These extreme examples make the point that a truly mobilised team pays attention to all team members equally, and while we live in an imperfect world where your team might go in and out of balance to respond to the demands of clients, market conditions, staff issues, illness etc, checking in on the overall balance of team workload is a worthwhile habit to build into your practices.

Let's talk about managing your team's emotional integrity as an act of care. We all influence each other. While it's important to avoid black-and-white rules like 'no negativity in our team', it's equally important to acknowledge the effect of one person's negativity on others around them. Have a chat with your team about emotional integrity within the work environment. Discuss the role of emotions in the team, how they help or hinder reading the environment, making decisions and achieving results and how your team want to deal with them. Share the Feeling Wheel from Chapter 2 with them. If your team was a character, what would the overall emotional signature of that character be? Daring? Inferior? Discouraged? Confident? Emotions are energy. What kind of energy best serves your mission? Remember, people look to you as a role model. You have to walk the talk.

Communicate

The Communicate pillar prioritises real and timely conversations. It is the realm of information sharing and expression.

You set the tone for communication in your team. Adopt a mindset that opens up possibilities and guides movement towards your goals. Encourage dialogue when there are difficulties. Dialogue is a particular kind of conversation that places relationship at its heart. It has great value when you want to understand what's going on with people and get to the truth so that you can base decisions on high-quality information. Open dialogue between you and your team facilitates clarity and accuracy of communication out into the wider organisation. This is important because it's the secrets, the 'can't tell, won't tells' within your business, that bring you down. Dialogue is a powerful means of resolution for teams in conflict. Done properly, the process allows each person to fully express their views and fully listen until a solution is reached. For dialogue to happen, you need inner steadiness. The presence it gives you generates trust and affects other people's ability to share openly.

Collaborate

The Collaborate pillar emphasises that you don't have to run the business single-handedly and make all the decisions alone. You know this, and yet when the pressure is on and something causes even a tiny rupture in trust, there's a temptation to begin to work alone or for your self-interest. This applies to you and any member of your team. It only takes one person to stop collaborating, and the team has stopped collaborating. Establishing principles and systems of collaboration enables the repairing of trust when inevitable conflicts and difficulties arise and helps you to step back because there is explicit agreement around ways of working. In your collaboration principles and systems, include agreements around sharing information to join the dots between your individual reads of the environment, how you will make big and small decisions and any other team-specific factors.

The outcome of the 3Cs is an environment where team members have a foundational stability that enables them to fly. People are motivated and work well together even though there might be things they don't like about each other. This is possible because they care and are willing to negotiate and resolve difficulties, and because there's good decision-making around the table. When you and your team model strong teamwork, others in the business can see how it's done and mimic it to expand the benefits.

Redefine success measures

Barriers arise and stick around because they are measured and rewarded. Measure what matters now. Reward what matters now. Naturally, what matters will change in transitional periods. Take the time and energy to translate what you stand for now into new behaviours. Best practice examples help people understand what good and bad look like and practically guide your people on what to do in work situations.

A business that rewards the behaviours and outcomes it wants to be repeated builds alignment in real time.

Rewarding behaviours and outcomes that go against the values of the organisation, or are at odds with its purpose, mission or vision, creates disconnect, incoherence and confused people.

Take decision-making in your business, for example. What behaviours are you wanting to see from your team members? Are these rewarded? Is there training and coaching to support people to learn and apply the skills underpinning them? Do the systems and processes enable these behaviours or get in the way of them? What are you rewarding that doesn't support you to build a stable, aligned environment where better decisions can be made? If you say you want your team to speak up when they notice unusual behaviour that could influence future choices and decisions, but then diminish and penalise them for doing so, it won't take long for people to stop speaking up when they have a hunch that something is off.

If you reward individual performance that comes at the expense of sharing important information, don't be surprised if your team becomes a group of individuals making decisions out of self-interest rather than functioning as a true team. Your thought leadership and the example you set in redefining success measures can fast-track people-change initiatives throughout the whole of your business.

In Chapter 5 we identified performance management as a system in need of a revamp. What if leadership success measures now included components of the IRON framework? Imagine a business with KPIs around inner steadiness, reading the environment, overcoming challenges and never being done.

What if 'dynamic stability' became a new skills category, with measures like:

- Consistently demonstrates that stability comes from within

- Reads the team and business environment skilfully and accurately

- Shows ease and leadership in periods of prolonged uncertainty

- Handles the tensions of leadership in a volatile, complex world

- Makes wise, timely decisions

What if these measures were part of a system that had moved beyond the constraining language of 'performance management' and into the freeing language of 'potential realisation'? What if remuneration followed these kinds of metrics? What quality of leaders and organisations would such a system create?

What you measure and reward has an immense impact on your organisation. A new workplace landscape needs new measures. While the above conversation may not align with where your business is currently, it's a prompt to take a step back and get clear on what you're measuring and rewarding, and the consequences of this.

Continuous review

Continuous review of chosen success measures in teamwork, projects, decision-making and your leadership gives ongoing real-time information as you move forward. In today's world, leaders who prioritise continual review are in a strong position to keep their organisation stable as it changes, spot when a shift in direction is needed and realise their own leadership potential.

Intention is key in continuous review. Think about the culture you want to create in your team, business and inner world. Continuous review intent on controlling people or finding fault tends to create environments of fear. Stress levels rise, with all the associated costs at personal and business levels. Continuous review intent on realising potential and helping people grow moves you into the fertile territory of a learning environment, as we talked about in Chapter 3.

The size of your organisation will govern the level of complexity in your continuous review processes. Sometimes a simple approach is the most effective. The Shewhart/Deming four-stage cycle of Plan-Do-Check-Act (or Adjust) gives a basic framework for continuous review that you can modify for your context.[42] In your reviews, pay attention to factors that influence the stability of movement and look out for interconnections across different areas of your business.

Things take time to ripen. Continual review doesn't mean continual decisions and actions. It means continual noticing/listening and evaluating, until such time that decisions and action are needed. It's another expression of reading the environment.

What's essential in all the approaches we've discussed in this chapter on how to move beyond challenges, whether it's your relationship with uncertainty, personal traps and tensions, team-related barriers or organisational blocks, is accessing your inner steadiness. From that vantage point, you offer stability to all the moving parts within and outside of you.

CASE STUDY: Oliver leaps forward with the 3Cs, honest self-reflection and reappraisal

Back to Oliver. This is what he did to move forward. First, he organised a day off-site with his team to reconnect with them as a priority. Taking each pillar of the 3Cs Team Mobiliser Model in turn, the team applied it in their context.

The results included renewed enthusiasm and energy for the mission of the business and a discovery that the CTO was doing the work of one and a half people and needed some support. The team resolved a misunderstanding that was affecting morale, found a way for the CFO to trial working at home three days a week for the next three months and finally agreed on principles for decision-making that gave clarity about the decisions that belonged to individuals and those that belonged to the team.

The input of the interim CMO on the day was invaluable. It turned out that the role wasn't working for her, either. Through respectful dialogue, she agreed to head up the recruitment of a permanent replacement and Oliver agreed to set aside a budget for a coach to help her find her next position.

Oliver also reconsidered his polarised stance on a 'full-time, office-based' replacement CMO and realised that fear was driving his attitude. Through honest self-reflection and assessing various scenarios, his perception changed and he became open to new ways of working.

A breakthrough for them all was asking 'What's the opportunity in this uncertainty?' This question opened up new possibilities for the direction of the business and the team's ways of working, and for each of them personally. Once back in the office, Oliver privately began his search for a coach who worked across life and leadership to help him make some of the big decisions he needed to make.

CHAPTER EXERCISE: Just 10 minutes, Part Three

Sit (or walk) for just 10 minutes at the end of each day, for three consecutive days, and reflect on:

- Three moments where your choices, actions or habits were a barrier to your inner steadiness, your read of the environment or your tenacity in overcoming challenges
- Three moments when you weren't the leader you wanted to be
- Three actions your wisest self invites you to take tomorrow in response to your new insights

Don't forget to draw on self-compassion when you need it. You can make this exercise a practice by doing it on an ongoing basis.

Summary

You can move beyond challenges by:

- Relaxing into uncertainty
- Using mind-body freedom techniques to loosen and release thinking traps and navigate leadership tensions
- Mobilising your team with the 3Cs – Care, Communicate and Collaborate

- Redefining the success measures in your leadership, team and business

- Continuously reviewing teamwork, projects, decisions and your leadership

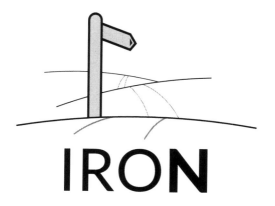

IRON

PART FOUR
NEVER DONE

You've so far worked through the first three parts of the IRON pathway to stability. You now have what you need to maintain a strong, calm inner steadiness in turbulence to tap into what's really going on in the environment around and within you and to navigate challenges to stability in a world of relentless change – but you're not done. You, me, your team, all of us, never are. An attitude of 'never done' becomes a safe and exciting thing when it co-exists with inner steadiness and the ability to read the environment and overcome challenges. It ensures that the stability within you, your team and your organisation becomes a dynamic launchpad towards your goals.

In Part Four, your pathway opens into an invitation to keep on making aligned choices for your ongoing evolution. Chapter 7 offers you a foundation for better decision-making that moves you, your team and your organisation towards the greatest potential and possibilities. Chapter 8 looks at the fruits of stability and what's possible for you and your business now you're operating from a foundation of dynamic stability.

SEVEN

The Vital Five-Element Foundation For Better Decision-Making

'All human activity is a matter of motion
and decision.'
—Frank Bunker Gilbreth, Sr[43]

While decision-making is simply the process of making a choice, it often isn't easy. We saw in Chapter 3 how complicated it can be in the organisational world. Modern leadership demands that you diligently examine reality while bravely creating the future through your decision-making. It requires your willingness to be both a scientist and an artist. A fast route to instability is to make reactive choices that create division; to move forward with stability, make decisions that unify.

A foundation is an essential starting point, especially for the big decisions. This chapter is about laying a foundation for better decision-making in a transitional world that pulls you from pillar to post. Through five key elements, you establish a launchpad from which to choose a way forward based on your greatest potential, which always unifies.

The foundation is 'vital' in both senses of the word. It's essential *and* it generates energy. Just as iron reduces fatigue and enables the transmission of oxygen to the farthest parts of your body, the five elements we'll learn about in this chapter support you in making decisions that transmit life outwards into your overall system.

The elements aren't a decision-making model. They are the ingredients of a platform from which to make balanced and integrated choices that move you towards a future you want to be part of. Think of the elements as forming a living, breathing space that supports you to flourish and flow. Weaving together threads of this book, they rest on your inner steadiness, rely on your ability to read your environment and need your courage and persistence to move beyond inner challenges and ensure you're heading towards your goals.

The foundation also gives you an agreed basis for decisions across your team that generates awareness and builds trust because you are all adopting the same principles when making your choices.

The five elements are:

1. Stating the decision
2. Understanding inner movements
3. Building on strengths
4. Embodying what you stand for
5. Prioritising wellbeing

Each element is a crucial part of the whole. They aren't discrete and their sequence isn't necessarily linear. They work together and iteratively reveal things to help you make choices that are felt, deep and true, rather than coming from surface-level thinking or unknown fears. When laying your foundation, you might make discoveries that give you the clarity you need to make a change without a lengthy decision-making process. Happy days. Go ahead and make that decision. Or you might experience the opposite. The fourth element might reveal an important previously missed aspect that changes the first element, the decision you are making.

Let's walk through the elements together now.

Element 1: Stating the decision

Decisions can emerge from reading your inner and outer environment. They can be imposed upon you by key stakeholders or be a natural crossroads inviting you and your business to move to the next phase.

Sometimes, clearly stating a decision that you are making is easy, and the first element of your foundation is in place swiftly. Other times, it isn't straightforward. Complexity clouds the situation and your thinking. It's hard to frame and articulate the choice you face. When you find it tricky to state a decision, whether team, business or life-related, get out a pen, paper, flipchart or laptop, and write freely about it – don't worry about preciseness. Involve others as appropriate. Describe it in whatever way you can. Include key aspects that seem important to you at this point.

Consider these questions to scope your decision:

- What need, challenge or opportunity does this decision address?

- What is the goal of the decision? What do you want to accomplish through making it?

- What is the scale of the decision? For example, is it an organisational restructure or a mini experiment in a new market? Is it a major life redesign or a small step in a new direction?

If words are not forthcoming, draw your decision, mind-map it, use AI software to help you – do whatever you can to connect with it and express it. Now look back at what you have written, drawn or discovered and summarise your decision as best you can right now.

Once stated, stay open to what may be revealed as you build more of your foundation. Be willing to adjust your words and understanding of the decision as needed. Don't get attached to what you think the answer will be.

Element 2: Understanding inner movements

The second element is about identifying and understanding the significant and sometimes differing internal movements you have in relation to the decision: the inner challenges of your fears, traps and tensions we talked about in Part Three, alongside the inner motivators of your hopes and desires.

Inner movements are energy. They are the invisible fuel that turbo-charges you towards your goal and to who you (and your business) are or leads you into a wilderness of stagnation and confusion, and away from who you are. At an organisational systems level, inner movements can play out in the various agendas, needs and priorities within your organisation.

Some leaders are surprised when I ask them to consider their deeper inner world in relation to a business decision. What has that got to do with deciding whether to buy a company, reduce your prices or restructure the business? After twenty-plus years of coaching, I can tell you: a lot.

First, it prevents unconscious decision-making. Put another way, it uncovers the real motivations for your choices and actions. There's often a lot happening inside that we don't acknowledge in a work context, even to ourselves. Element 2 encourages you to build a decision-making foundation based on self-awareness.

Bring openness and curiosity to the range of reactions and responses that arise in you concerning a decision. Perhaps you have already started to jump into, or back away from, some options. Inner conflict might be pulling you in different directions. Two important values might seem to be at odds with each other, creating an 'I don't know what to do' thinking loop.

We talk about embodying what you stand for in Element 4. This is what gives you alignment in your decision-making. If inner movements get in the way, we aren't free to embody what we stand for. We're trapped in unconscious inner fears or conflicting desires. The more invested in the status quo you are, the harder it is to see these movements (in yourself and your organisation) clearly and without bias. Even more reason, then, to seek to understand what's going on inside.

If you're focusing on understanding inner movements rather than denying them, when the skeletons in that cupboard show themselves and attempt to derail you through, for example, their voices of doubt and perfectionism, telling you that you're not good enough, not worthy enough, not [fill in the blank] enough, you won't be fazed. You'll be wise to their line of attack on your identity ('you can't do it. Who do you think you are? You'll fail') or that of the organisation ('we're second tier, not in the same league as X. Who'd want to work here? We can't risk that').

You know that listening to these inner critics blocks healthy innovation, necessary risk-taking and a daring that you'll need to move into a new phase in your business, leadership and life. Realising that they are a normal part of leading and being human helps you to treat them kindly but firmly as you move beyond them to steady your foundation and see your different options and the way forward more clearly.

Understanding your inner movements also helps you grow as a leader. You gain clarity about your process and get closer to expressing your full potential, which has immense benefits for the business and those around you. You are more honest with yourself and don't shy away from the discomfort that inner movements can bring. You are alert to the dangers of avoidance, and keen to perceive conflicting pulls as opportunities for growth. This gives you the motivation for the often hard work of sifting through inner tensions and contradictions, understanding their source and finding the way through.

Consciously bringing your deepest hopes and fears for yourself, others and humanity into the choices you encounter in your work and life can be challenging and transformational. It's not how things are traditionally done in the business world, where logic and rationality reign. There's no denying these are important qualities but without a heartfelt connection to the decision in its entire trajectory, important human factors and consequences can be disregarded in ignorance. Getting inwardly close to a substantial decision takes courage. It's easier to keep yourself at arm's length in an unconscious bid for self-protection, and unwittingly betray your deeper self, your mission and others.

Finally (and crucially), if you understand your inner movements, you make better decisions. You don't have to resolve every fear, trap and tension or achieve every identified desire and hope. This would be unrealistic. If you simply stay with your inner landscape, seeking understanding and alignment, until you reach a point of internal equilibrium, then your decisions will be true.

Being wise to your inner movements enables you to resist making decisions when you're in the grip of fear or overly excited. You know your foundation isn't ready (or steady) and the message is to wait until you have more understanding about what is happening inside. If you hit the wall of loneliness that can appear when you are seeking to make choices and lead towards something genuinely new, you know to allow it and move through it. If you are being asked to make a key decision while you're experiencing inner turmoil, you know to get support from trusted others to make it well.

It can take time to work through your experiences of inner movements and reach equilibrium. It isn't something to be rushed just to get through it. It's an opportunity to deepen your understanding of yourself, your context, the organisation and the decision you face. Of course, in the busy day-to-day with continual pressure for speed, this principle can be difficult to adhere to, but it's worth it because the alternative of making decisions from a place of unexamined motivations and ways of thinking rarely leads to good outcomes. The inner work you do to sift and move through fears, traps, tensions, hopes and desires will change and build you into a leader who can deal with difficulty and difference, discern which ambitions to follow and generate a sense of togetherness.

Sometimes there is a genuine stillness within in relation to a decision. This inner freedom to choose means Element 2 is already stable in your foundation. Wonderful. Move on and nourish your other foundational elements.

Element 3: Building on strengths

It's easy to lose touch with what you're good at under the pressures of deciding and delivering. Reminding yourself of your strengths and anchoring into them gives you an immediate resource to navigate inner movements and make aligned choices. The decision-making process overall is likely to be easier, and the outcome of a decision better, when you're building on your strengths. Bring the best of your decision-making style to the context of the choice you are making, and factor in the role of your strengths in securing a positive outcome over the long term.

We already mentioned Gallup's CliftonStrengths when we looked at your decision-making personality in Chapter 1. If you didn't explore this at the start of the book, don't have a language for your strengths or simply want a reminder, take a look now. It is one of several online psychometric tools you can draw on to ensure your decision-making foundation is strengthened by your innate talents.

The need to build on strengths also applies to your team and organisation. What are they naturally good at? How can these qualities be built upon? This doesn't mean ignoring weaknesses; it means moving in a strengths-based direction where there is greater natural flow. For collaborative decisions, make sure you've got the right people around the table with a mix of strengths, to make the best choice.

Element 4: Embodying what you stand for

In decision-making, context is everything. Knowing and embodying what you stand for instantly puts your decision-making into the right context. It points to the bigger picture of your choices: your values, core beliefs and guiding principles; your purpose, mission and vision. This is about your identity as a leader and business. Without this context, it's easy to get caught in problems and disappear under a mountain of options.

If you want to get laser-focused, home in on the one core belief underpinning your whole business. With that level of clarity, the signpost for decisions becomes a neon light. Take, for example, a core belief of 'We can break new ground with our thinking.' Everyone in your team and the business knows exactly what they're about from that one statement, and it becomes the guiding principle at the heart of their decisions.

Or you might choose to focus on your values and mission to guide you. Core values of connection, inspiration and learning, and a mission of 'justice for all' give you a strong compass in any decision-making situation.

However you describe what you stand for, it is an expression of your deepest aspirations, of who you want to be and what you want to achieve in the world.

They become the goal and the marker in decision-making. Get clear on this and choices become a lot easier. Asking 'Will this move me towards my vision/mission or away from it?' can give you clarity quickly. If multiple stakeholders stand for different things to you and demand compromise in a decision, return to Element 4 of your foundation and consciously choose what you will (and will not) compromise on. It's not necessarily about getting to your desired outcome as fast as possible. The most compelling and relevant vision/mission in an organisation may be unachievable in one person's lifetime.

When you are faced with a difficult choice, being in a state of equilibrium and connected with what you stand for gives you the strongest foundation from which to decide. This is especially important when people could be hurt or negatively affected by an option that is on the table. Knowing that some higher good will come from going down that route can give you the courage to make the brave choice if you sense it's needed.

Given the transitional era we are in, it's essential to revisit and consciously update your values, purpose, vision etc so that you don't make decisions based on old data. When you don't know what you stand for or are still attached to the version of your mission that was relevant twenty years ago, you can flounder in a no man's land of indecision or make choices based on an outdated foundation or one that belongs to other people (and organisations) and does not reflect who and what you are now.

Element 5: Prioritising wellbeing

Prioritising wellbeing can be challenging for many in leadership. It's the thing that happens after everything else if there's time. But here's the rub: your decision-making suffers when you neglect your wellbeing. Your wellbeing affects your attitude and the quality of your decisions. You are your most important resource when it comes to choosing well.

Supporting your own wellbeing means taking care of all aspects of yourself. This includes your mind, body, heart and spirit. It's important at any time, but when you've got a multitude of novel (for you) decisions to make, having the energy to fully engage is essential.

Many of us speed up in the face of big decisions. It can be a form of avoidance. You get ahead of yourself, literally. The head takes over and you leave the heart, body and spirit behind. The result is you get tired, unwell and less able to make wise decisions. When you know the pattern, you can act against it and deliberately slow down.

Though it might seem counterintuitive, rest is an essential component of your decision-making foundation. Almost every leader I have ever worked with (including myself) has a complicated relation-ship with rest. Ask yourself now: when was the last time you experienced meaningful rest that truly nourished you?

When you support your wellbeing, you create the inner conditions for skilful and wise decision-making. The below practices can help you.

DAILY PRACTICE: Honouring the basics of self-care

Every day, support your nervous system and your wellbeing by eating a balanced diet that is low in sugar and caffeine, drinking plenty of water, doing 30 minutes of gentle exercise,[44] laughing, finding things in your day to be grateful for[45] and building healthy sleep habits that mean you wake refreshed.

DAILY PRACTICE: Balancing receiving and giving support

Leaders are often in a support deficit, giving more than they are receiving. Organise your life and leadership so that you can receive emotional support from friends and loved ones, and practical support from professionals in the fields of wellbeing and wise decision-making. Ask yourself every day 'Am I receiving the support I need to lead and choose well?'

> **WEEKLY PRACTICE: Keeping a wellbeing scorecard**
>
> At the end of every week, give yourself a high, medium or low score for the wellness of your mind, body, heart and spirit. Take action to address areas that need more love. Don't forget to celebrate the progress of scores moving upwards.

When you have committed to a decision from the launchpad of your foundation, the combined power of all the elements places you in a strong position to engage in the action now required and be responsive to what emerges.

What's exciting about the Vital Five-Element Foundation is that you can use it as a perennial resource to keep your platform for decision-making up to date and relevant. Life and business are a cycle of ongoing evolution. With IRON as your companion, imagine what's possible.

CASE STUDY: Nina and her team build a decision-making foundation

Engagement had consistently come up in Nina's weekly meetings with her leadership team. Six of the seven faces around the table were noticing worryingly apathetic behaviours in their own teams and across the wider business since the change in ownership six months previously. It was clear that some decisions needed to be made.

The team spent time defining the problem and articulated their current understanding of the decision as 'choosing the best course of action to increase engagement'. Nina sensed another restructuring was the way forward and felt compassion for everyone at the further upheaval this would entail in the short term. She allowed the team to voice their hopes and fears about the decision. Everyone felt worried about the resilience of the workforce (and themselves) to further change. They also recognised that the status quo trap could be affecting their ability to think freely and clearly, as many of them were attached to the way the business was structured under its founders. There were tensions and disagreements about timing (act now versus wait) and finances (save versus spend). Discussing things together and gaining more understanding about their differing perspectives helped to clear and unify their thinking.

The team's reputation for discipline was a core strength they knew would help them in the decision-making process and the follow-through. Sticking to their values of care, service and integrity guided their thinking and would also help them deal with some of the push-back they might get from long-serving staff members in making further changes in the business. Nina knew the team were tired (as was she) and together they agreed on a 'Taking Care of Ourselves' pact. They'd done this before when the chips were down and it had provided an invaluable boost to their wellbeing.

Nina and her team felt steady going into the decision-making process because they had a strong foundation. There was a lot of work to do in gathering data, reviewing options and preparing a proposal for the new owners, but they'd ticked off the vital five elements on their decision-making foundation checklist and this gave them confidence. A good decision outcome looked likely. We'll meet Nina again at the end of Chapter 8 to see what happened.

CHAPTER EXERCISE: Building your foundation for better decision-making

To begin working on your decision-making foundation, take a moment to:

- Identify and state clearly a key upcoming personal, professional or business decision

- Name three hopes and three fears that you have concerning the decision right now

- Describe three essential aspects of what you stand for that you can use to guide you in your decision-making

Summary

The Vital Five-Element Foundation for Better Decision-Making comprises:

1. Stating the decision

2. Understanding inner movements

3. Building on strengths

4. Embodying what you stand for

5. Prioritising wellbeing

EIGHT

What's Possible Now?

'Why, sometimes I've believed as many as six
impossible things before breakfast.'
—Lewis Carroll[46]

When you have inner steadiness, can read the
environment, overcome challenges and have
a decision-making foundation you can rely on, the
realm of what's possible expands. Can you remember
a time when you woke up one day, free of some bur-
den or a worry that had been weighing you down?
Lighter and liberated, you see clearly what to do.
A decision that may have seemed impossible, you
now make in a heartbeat. After months of delibera-
tion, the future comes towards you at speed. Anything seems possible.

In our final chapter, we look at the fruits of stability: true confidence in the direction of the business, a team working as one, the capacity to keep on changing and the centredness to keep your finger on the pulse of what brings you alive as a person and a leader. We started the book with you, and we close with you too. Having been on this journey, what's next for you?

Confidence in your direction

Have you ever seen Monty Python's 'Silly Olympics: Race for people with no sense of direction'?[47] It's a short video of eight runners beginning a 100-yard race on an athletics track. As they prepare to take their positions at the beginning of the race, the runners pace around, psych themselves up to give it their best shot, crouch down into position on the start line and then – bang – the starting pistol is fired. At that moment, instead of running in the same direction towards their destination, they all run off in different directions and there is disarray. Aside from being amusing, the vignette is a powerful visual demonstration of people choosing to participate in a race, while being unaware of or disinterested in the aim of that race. What none of us knows is the individual motivations of those runners and the bigger story they were part of. What we do know is that these things were not strong enough to focus their direction.

With the Stability Effect, you don't have to fear that you and your team will be running off in different directions at the start of every day, dissipating energy and forward momentum. The bigger story of your organisation, expressed through what you stand for, generates a magnetic field that aligns people and guides them to face in the same direction and to work together towards common goals. With IRON at the core of your leadership and a real-time stable decision-making foundation in place, you can trust that your aims have integrity and your direction is true. There's a confidence in you (and your team) that can only come from knowing that your choices and actions flow from a storyline that pulls you together as one.

Working as one

I had the unexpected joy of experiencing a team pulling together as one while having my hair cut one autumnal Saturday. As I sat there explaining to the hairdresser what I wanted, I first heard, then saw, a Rock Choir outside the salon window, singing a series of uplifting songs. With hours of practice under their belt, that Saturday afternoon the choir worked harmoniously together to blend their voices and create a cohesive sound that delighted the audience and passers-by. Each choir member had a specific role to play in creating a beautiful performance.

We see the same cohesion and excellence when a football team is in flow. It seems like the players are reading each other's minds and know where each is going to be before the ball is kicked. The mid-fielder reads the environment of the pitch and opens possibilities with a long ball to the left wing. Two moves later, the ball is in the back of the net.

In nature, bees work together as one to maintain the stability of their community and gather resources for growth. These social creatures each have specific roles and responsibilities. The queen bee is responsible for laying eggs. Worker bees perform tasks like building the hive, caring for the young and gathering nectar and pollen. Honeybee communication arises through their socially learned 'waggle dance', which shares information with other bees in the colony about the location of food, allowing them to find and collect resources quickly.[48]

In organisational life, the dream is that all teams want to, and can, work seamlessly together, being clear on their roles and responsibilities, building on individual strengths yet remaining unified in their approach. They will make choices that serve the current priorities and aims of the business and the workforce, with an individual mindset of 'How can I improve myself?' being replaced with one of 'How can we become more together?'

While such perfection of mindset and action is rare in real life, especially in larger organisations where there can be hundreds of teams working towards alignment, it's a worthy aspiration and demands an inner resolve and consistency of effort that the IRON process can give you.

Realising full potential and achieving the impossible is greatly aided by learning from someone you admire and aspire to be like. In his book *Fortitude*, Bruce Daisley names Liverpool Football Club manager Jürgen Klopp as a role model who favours collective identity over singular leadership.[49] Klopp's sense of 'us' went beyond the players to include support staff and supporters. His behaviours followed his principles. He learned the names of everyone who worked at the club's training ground and introduced each one on the stage of the press conference room, to the players' applause. He also made known his dissatisfaction with Liverpool supporters leaving games early when the team was losing. In Klopp's mind, this was not working as one.

When you achieve the Stability Effect, you and your team can become role models for working as one in your organisation, showing others what it looks, sounds and feels like, and the impact of such cohesion. This doesn't negate the necessity of having your own role model; in fact, it makes it even more important as a sustaining practice.

WEEKLY PRACTICE: Following a role model

Find a role model who inspires and stretches you with their purpose and actions. You might find this person in your physical network. Or they might be a public figure who you can follow on social media. Maybe they passed away centuries ago. Wherever they come from, listen to and read their words of wisdom. Learn by their example. To make this a focused effort, choose one quality per week that you admire and emulate it.

Keep on changing

'It is in changing that we find purpose.'[50] This ancient wisdom is said to be that of Heraclitus of Ephesus, who seems to be urging us to keep changing to live a life of meaning. For organisations, an absence of desire to continue changing renders a stable organisation just that, stable. There's no pull forward, or growth and movement, in that type of stability. It becomes a stagnant pool and misses the opportunity to grow into a vibrant flowing stream full of life, which can become a powerful river moving with energy towards the vast ocean.

When outside circumstances force you to change, you can become overly protective and hunker down, simply trying to survive. You become rigid without realising it. The four-part IRON pathway guards against this and helps you (your team and your organisation) to keep changing and growing with more ease than would otherwise be possible.

It also helps you to change with the right timing. In this respect, it's helpful to understand the difference between Chronos (chronological or sequential) time and Kairos (opportune or right) time. Your financial year end is governed by Chronos time. It's fixed, repeats every year and doesn't care about context. Other, more fluid events like beginning new initiatives, launching new products and services, taking holidays and changing roles, organisations or careers are governed by Kairos time, where context is crucial and there is an optimum or critical moment for decision and action. Learn how to read the environment (within you and outside of you) and you learn how to flow with Kairos time; you master the art of changing at the right time.

Sometimes this means speed. Fast choice and action are needed. Other times, it is slowness that reaps rewards. The enemies of Kairos time are rigid timelines, blinkered perspectives, a denial of the systemic process of change (and life) and a refusal to reflect and learn. When a leader imposes unrealistic expectations on a product launch, for instance. It's like making a tree shed its leaves in summer out of time with its surroundings. Some leaders are wise to the significance of Kairos time and may go so far as to seek astrological input to get as close to the perfect constellation as humanly possible.

You might have noticed that the undertone of this book is about moving business leaders towards wholeness. Never being done isn't always about achieving more, but it is always about *becoming* more. This is hard to realise without the rub of change. That's why embracing change, even when it's relentless and feels hard, is an invitation we want to accept. When we embrace change co-creatively, both making decisions that shape it and allowing ourselves to be shaped by it, we continuously grow and evolve.

As you change, bear in mind the poor track record in organisations for recognising and celebrating success. Harvard professor Teresa Amabile and independent researcher Steven Kramer discovered the power of celebrating even small wins at work. Their review of the inner world diaries of employees was the inspiration behind what is now called the Progress Principle.[51] According to the principle, when leaders take time to acknowledge people's progress in work that matters to them, the positive effect on wellbeing, motivation and creative output is significant. When applying this principle within the 'Keep on changing' requirement of the Stability Effect, the message is to continue appreciating how far you (and your team) have come and find visible ways to celebrate that.

Finger on the pulse

The 'Just 10 minutes' reflective exercises at the end of the second chapter in each part of this book have been designed to help keep your finger on the pulse of the theme of each part. They have been intentionally succinct, giving you just enough information to extract value from the activity. There is another such exercise at the end of this chapter focusing on what energises you, which is crucial information in determining your choices and actions for the future.

As we approach the end of our time together in this book, it feels like the right moment to share a more comprehensive reflective exercise called the structured daily review that reveals the potential for deeper contemplation. You can adopt this as a practice that you do every day to keep your finger on the pulse of what's important in your leadership and life overall and plug you into the flow of Kairos time.

DAILY PRACTICE: Structured daily review

There are many ways to do this review, depending on what you want to achieve. The format offered here guides you to listen to what's important in your reality, spot changes brewing on the horizon, know when decisions are ready to be made and claim actions that are there for the taking.

When this kind of review is built into your life, you have a trusted tool to help you keep on changing

---

in line with your deepest desires and highest potential. You can tweak it for your own context and personality. The version that follows assumes you do the review in the evening, but you could do it first thing in the morning and reflect on the day before. However you do it, make this review work for you.

Preparation

To physically mark the beginning of your review, sit down, light a candle, close your book/notepad/laptop or even step outside and go for a walk. Get quiet and centred. Gather your attention from all the places you've left it during the day and spend a moment being thankful for some aspect of your experience, big or small. This preparation sets you up for openness. Otherwise, you tend to only see what you think you already know in your review.

Review

When you feel composed, begin your review. Ask your wisest self to show you the most important moment of your day, the moment that had the biggest impact on you or others, whether that impact was emotional, mental, physical or spiritual. Your review isn't about looking at every event in your day; it's about identifying those that had some level of significance for you.

When you have chosen a moment, consider why it was important. What was happening? What were you thinking? How were you feeling? What about deep down, how were you feeling there? Can you remember any physical sensations, such as what was going on in your body or how your posture and breathing were? What were the consequences of that moment?

If you have the time and appetite for it, ask your wisest self to identify another important moment or moments and repeat the above reflections.

Look to tomorrow

Now look to tomorrow and ask yourself what you think will be your most important moment. What do you want to happen in that moment? Who do you need to be in that moment to bring this about?

If you have the time and appetite, identify another moment or moments tomorrow that you think will be important and repeat the above questions.

Close

To close your review, make a concrete resolution to be the kind of leader and person you want to be and identify any action you wish to take tomorrow to bring this about. If making notes helps you capture the key elements of your experience. Physically mark the end of your review by standing up or blowing out the candle.

The most basic result of your review is that you will become more connected with yourself and your experience. This alone is payback for your time. In addition, more nuanced rewards will emerge over days and months if your practice of reflection is sustained, including clarity about your feelings, thoughts, deeper desires and awareness of themes, patterns, ongoing motives and interests. As you develop through this ongoing review, you will become increasingly skilled at identifying habits you want to reinforce or change and decisions that need to be made. You can discern and choose the better way forward, and plan and act with the right timing.

Even if you can't do the review daily, a regular reflective practice will protect you from reaching the end of the year and saying 'There's another year of my life (or business) I can't get back.' The psychiatrist Carl Jung claimed that after age thirty-five every emotional crisis arises because of a crisis of meaning.[52] Reflecting daily on what's been important in your day keeps meaning close and crises at bay, unable to get a foothold.

What's next for you?

Working in an organisation is like being in a relationship. The organisation changes and you change. This is natural and as it should be. The key to living purposefully is spotting when there's no longer a match. Then it's time to make decisions for change.

Perhaps the organisational mission doesn't align with your value system anymore, or the enjoyment has gone for you. Maybe your motivation for leading is changing and you're being called into a new phase. An activity that was on the periphery of your life might now have more significance and meaning, and you want to devote more time to it. Perhaps the organisation needs a new leadership style that isn't who you are. Or you might simply need a new challenge.

With your skills and capabilities, there are many avenues you could take, some within the business and some beyond it. When you sense the time is ripe for change, whether next week, next month, next year or in three years, alongside your daily review (and not just at the end of a bad day or week) carve out time and space to consider what's next for you. Ask yourself what motivated you to get to the top and what your ambition is currently. Reflect on what leadership means to you now and discern whether your purpose is changing. What is it that you truly want at this point in your life and work? How do you want to feel?

These probing questions can be difficult to answer immediately. They invite you to connect deep inside and let go of outdated external expectations, and take hold of a truer, more current expression of what you stand for. Let that guide you. Articulate it, tune into it, feel it, choose it and live it.

You can apply everything we've talked about in *The Stability Effect* in your personal life or career. Take yourself through the four parts of IRON again with this new focus. You might consider taking a retreat day to think things through properly and prevent planning for your future from slipping to the bottom of your to-do list. There are many activities you can do on that day, including creating a vision of your ideal future and meeting your future self.

The key to staying fulfilled is to keep changing and evolving. Your life is an adventure that change facilitates. With the strength of IRON behind you, what's next for you?

CASE STUDY: Nina is ready for her next adventure

Let's now return to Nina's situation. A decision to restructure the business was made and implemented with great success. Staff engagement has risen and the financial metrics are keeping everyone happy. Six months on and the leadership team have moved into a new gear, confident in the direction the business is going and in themselves as a key part of it. Nina, meanwhile, is wondering whether her work in the business is done. She feels strong and steady inside, in tune with her clients, team and the new business owners. A part of her is tempted to simply enjoy the fruits of her labour for the next year, five years or even until retirement. She's worked hard to reach this place. Despite this, she feels a restlessness for change.

Nina began practising a daily review as part of her process for deciding to restructure. She found it so valuable that she continued once the decision was made, using it as a reliable way to stay connected with her experience. Her days are full of action and 10 minutes of purposeful reflection each day helps her stay on track with what is important.

Over the past three months, she has noticed a repeated theme arising in her daily reviews about the importance to her of nature, in particular rivers and the sea. She took this awareness into a retreat day. In the space created by the retreat, she imagined her life five years in the future and her whole body knew that she would be working in some way to protect rivers or the sea, and the creatures that live there. She feels deeply excited about this possibility. Nina knows she'll never be done changing and growing, and she finds joy in that as she considers her next step to making her vision a reality.

CHAPTER EXERCISE: Just 10 minutes, Part Four

Sit (or walk) for just 10 minutes at the end of each day, for three consecutive days, and reflect on:

- Three moments where you felt energised
- What this might mean for you
- Three actions your wisest self invites you to take tomorrow in response to your new insights

You can make this exercise a practice by doing it on an ongoing basis.

Summary

What's possible expands when:

- You have confidence in your direction
- Your team are working as one
- You are willing to change and evolve
- You keep your finger on the pulse of what brings you alive
- You work towards fulfilling your mission in life

Conclusion

C hange is an all-encompassing aspect of life. If we didn't acknowledge this before the global Covid-19 pandemic, we need to acknowledge it now. At the time of writing, the world, workplaces and leadership are transforming – visibly, viscerally and rapidly – before our eyes. Even when change is this relentless, and many things seem out of our control, we have a choice about the way we engage in the process. What will you choose? The hard way, or the easy way?

Hard or easy?

Choosing the hard way is choosing the old way. Nothing changes in how we approach change. Organisations and people continue to feel anxious inside.

We ignore reality. We deny change, fight it, impose on it, resist it and hold onto what we know. We compete and attempt to control. We make decisions reactively, out of fear, based on outdated information, irrelevant ideas and a head that is disconnected from the heart and the wisdom of the body. Despair is high and learning is low. Leadership is ungrounded, fragmented, out of touch and privately afraid. Humanity is all over the place.

Choosing the easy way is choosing the new way. We evolve as organisations and people, open ourselves to the opportunities of change and feel steady inside. We collaborate and co-create. In the right relationship with our environment, we make decisions responsively and with integrity, using real-time information, new ideas and the integrated intelligence of a body that is settled, a mind that is open and a heart that is compassionate and strong. Despair is low and learning is high. Leadership is grounded, centred and embodied – an adventure. Humanity has a dynamic stability.

The Stability Effect has shown you how to move towards the easy way of approaching change in your leadership because the easy way is hard enough. My four-part pathway, IRON – Inner Steadiness, Reading The Environment, Overcoming Challenges and Never Done – will transform your experience.

PART ONE	PART TWO	PART THREE	PART FOUR
Inner Steadiness	Reading The Environment	Overcoming Challenges	Never Done
I	R	O	N

The IRON pathway

Within IRON, you can draw on the BBM model for inner steadiness, the 'Listen Out, Listen In' process to read your environment, the 3Cs Team Mobiliser Model, and the Vital Five-Element Foundation for Better Decision-Making.

I said in the introduction that I wrote this book because I've seen the struggle to get stability and change to co-exist and work together. The Stability Effect will ease this struggle. The sooner you start to walk the IRON pathway, the sooner you tap into the greatest resource you have, which is you and your centred connection within.

There will always be people who condemn inner work and remain uneasy about the reflection and discernment that are a core part of this book. However, reflection performed as a platform for action, and discernment made in service of your people and mission, cannot fail to move you forward in alignment and integrity.

The Stability Effect is a book of paradox. It is when you are steady and connected inside that you can connect more fully with people around you and your environ-ment. It is when you are strong in what you stand for that change can happen more gracefully than would otherwise be possible. It is when you have stability that ongoing change is attainable.

While *The Stability Effect* focuses on bringing forth the qualities that enable you to be a steady and consistently bright North Star of your business, its IRON process is transferable to other domains. A desire to realise their potential and move towards the life and world they want is at the heart of most of the conversations I have with people. This might reveal itself as a spe-cific question: how to make a wise decision, live a life of purpose and find more joy. Whatever the context, the way forward is found through inner steadiness, reading the environment, overcoming challenges and making the ongoing decisions that will move you towards your goal and becoming more you.

Thank you for the privilege of letting me walk you through the four parts of the IRON pathway. I hope you'll update me on your next steps and the impact of applying it in your leadership, business and life.

My IRON Training Programme

You've read the book, understood the practices suggested and done the awareness exercises at the end of each chapter. You're ready. The moment has come.

To keep the Stability Effect alive in your leadership and life, now is the time to build your IRON Training Programme of practices from each of the four parts of the IRON pathway.

Here's how:

1. Choose one daily or weekly practice from each of the four parts. (The index that follows will help you do that with ease.) Select the ones you believe will make the most significant difference

to you and your goals and insert them into the 'My IRON Training Programme' Month 1 template opposite.

2. Sign the programme and choose someone you trust and who can support your accountability to sign it as your witness.

3. Do the four practices for a month and mark your progress on the template with a tick.

4. When complete, ask your accountability partner to initial the completion dates.

5. Review the effect of your four practices and the progress you have made.

6. Choose four practices again. They could be the same ones as before or different, depending on your needs. Write them on a new monthly template and repeat the above process.

Continue your training on an ongoing basis. Stability, wise decision-making and realising your leadership and life potential arise from your day-to-day choices.

MY **IRON** TRAINING PROGRAMME
Month 1

The Practice	INNER STEADINESS [INSERT]	READING THE ENVIRONMENT [INSERT]	OVERCOMING CHALLENGES [INSERT]	NEVER DONE [INSERT]
Day 1	[tick as done]			
Day 2				
Day 3				
Day 4				
Day 5				
Day 6				
Day 7				
Day 8				
Day 9				
Day 10				
Day 11				
Day 12				
Day 13				
Day 14				
Day 15				
Day 16				
Day 17				
Day 18				
Day 19				
Day 20	.			
Day 21				
Day 22				
Day 23				
Day 24				
Day 25				
Day 26				
Day 27				
Day 28				
Day 29				
Day 30				

Leader: Witness:
Signature: Signature:

Start Date:
Completion Date:

Index Of IRON Practices

Inner steadiness

Reading the environment

Overcoming challenges

Never done

Notes

1   Linus Pauling Institute: Micronutrient
    Information Center, 'Iron' (Oregon State
    University, no date), https://lpi.oregonstate.edu/
    mic/minerals/iron, accessed September 2023
2   Socrates as quoted in Plato, *Plato in Twelve
    Volumes, Vol 1*, trans HN Fowler (William
    Heinemann Ltd, 1966)
3   T Eurich, *Insight: How to succeed by seeing yourself
    clearly* (Pan, 2018)
4   Harvard Medical School, 'Understanding the
    stress response' (Harvard Health Publishing,
    6 July 2020), www.health.harvard.edu/staying-
    healthy/understanding-the-stress-response,
    accessed 3 October 2023; NICABM, 'How
    to overcome the freeze response' (National
    Institute for the Clinical Application of

Behavioral Medicine, no date), www.nicabm. com/topic/freeze/, accessed 3 October 2023

5   K Drake, 'How the brain's "central alarm system" gathers threats and turns them into fear', *Medical News Today* (16 August 2022), www.medicalnewstoday.com/articles/how-the-brain-gathers-threat-cues-and-turns-them-into-fear, accessed 3 October 2023

6   D Rock, *Your Brain at Work: Strategies for overcoming distraction, regaining focus, and working smarter all day long* (HarperCollins, 2009)

7   E Kübler-Ross, *On Death and Dying: What the dying have to teach doctors, nurses, clergy and their own families* (Routledge, 2008)

8   D Dana, *The Polyvagal Theory in Therapy: Engaging the rhythm of regulation* (W. W. Norton & Company, 2018)

9   P King, 'Leadership Embodiment Training' (The Beyond Partnership, no date), www. thebeyondpartnership.co.uk, accessed September 2023

10 A Gopnik, *The Philosophical Baby: What children's minds tell us about truth, love and the meaning of life* (Bodley Head, 2009)

11 E Klein, 'Why adults lose the "beginner's mind"', The Ezra Klein Show (2021), https:// podcasts.apple.com/us/podcast/why-adults-lose-the-beginnersmind/id1548604447?i=10 00517373857&utm_source=substack&utm_medium=email, accessed September 2023

12 Rumi, *Selected Poems* (Penguin, 2015)
13 G Eliot, *Silas Marner* (Wordsworth Classics, 1994)
14 M Thorpe and R Ajmera, '12 science-based benefits of meditation' (Healthline, 27 October 2020), www.healthline.com/nutrition/12-benefits-of-meditation, accessed September 2023
15 A Olsson, *Conscious Breathing: Discover the power of your breath* (Sorena AB, 2014)
16 G Willcox, 'The Feeling Wheel', *Positive Psychology Practitioner's Toolkit* (PositivePsychology.com, no date), www.positivepsychology.com, accessed September 2023
17 T Eurich, *Insight: How to succeed by seeing yourself clearly* (Pan, 2018)
18 Confucius, *The Analects* (Penguin Classics, 1979)
19 EY, 'EY Future Workplace Survey' (Ernst & Young Global Limited, no date), www.ey.com/en_us/real-estate-hospitality-construction/ey-survey-on-future-workplace-index#item1, accessed September 2023
20 D Kolb, *Experiential Learning: Experience as the source of learning and development* (Prentice-Hall, 1984)
21 University of Edinburgh, 'Reflection Toolkit' (University of Edinburgh, 11 November 2020), www.ed.ac.uk/reflection/reflectors-toolkit/reflecting-on-experience/gibbs-reflective-cycle, accessed September 2023; G Gibbs, *Learning by Doing: A guide to teaching and learning methods* (FEU, 1988)

22 IM Verenikina and HM Hasan, 'The importance of play in organisation', *University of Wollongong Faculty of Health and Behavioural Sciences – Papers (Archive)* (2010), https://ro.uow.edu. au/cgi/viewcontent.cgi?referer=&httpsredir= 1&article=2823&context=hbspapers, accessed September 2023

23 AC Edmondson, 'Psychological safety, trust and learning: A group-level lens', in RM Kramer and KS Cook (Eds), *Trust and Distrust in Organizations: Dilemmas and approaches* (Russell Sage Foundation, 2004), 239–272

24 K Twaronite, 'The surprising power of simply asking coworkers how they're doing', *Harvard Business Review* (28 February 2019), https://hbr. org/2019/02/the-surprising-power-of-simply- asking-coworkers-how-theyre-doing, accessed September 2023

25 O Eastwood, *Belonging: Unlock your potential with the ancient code of togetherness* (Quercus, 2021)

26 K Mikkelsen and R Martin, *The Neo Generalist: Where you go is who you are* (LID Publishing, 2016)

27 See Amy C Edmondson's psychological safety 2×2 matrix model: https://amycedmondson. com/psychological-safety-%E2%89%A0- anything-goes/, accessed 9 October 2023

28 W Shakespeare, King Henry the Fourth, I, ii, 139

29 E Nymann, '12 animals that can supposedly predict the weather' (Weather Station Advisor,

2 October 2021), www.weatherstationadvisor. com/animals-that-can-predict-weather, accessed September 2023; ABC Science, 'Can animals predict the weather?' (ABC Science, 18 May 2010), www.abc.net.au/science/ articles/2010/05/18/2902595.htm, accessed September 2023

30 M Gladwell, *Blink: The power of thinking without thinking* (Penguin, 2006) pp122–123

31 M Boyle, 'Carly Fiorina talks tough', *CNN Money* (24 October 2007) https://money.cnn. com/2007/10/23/news/newsmakers/fiorina_ hp.fortune/index.htm, accessed 5 October 2023

32 F A Clark, *The Country Parson*, https://libquotes. com/frank-a-clark/quote/lbl8w6t, accessed 20 October 2023

33 M Lewis, 'Why we're hardwired to hate uncertainty', *The Guardian* (4 April 2016), www. theguardian.com/commentisfree/2016/apr/04/ uncertainty-stressful-research-neuroscience, accessed September 2023

34 DW Grupe and JB Nitschke, 'Uncertainty is associated with biased expectancies and heightened responses to aversion', *Emotion*, 11/2 (2011), 413–424, www.ncbi.nlm.nih.gov/pmc/ articles/PMC3086262/, accessed 4 October 2023

35 JS Hammond, RL Keeney and H Raiffa, 'The hidden traps in decision making', *Harvard Business Review* (September–October 1998), https://hbr.org/1998/09/the-hidden-traps-in-decision-making-2, accessed September 2023

36   M Aurelius, *Meditations: A new translation* (Modern Library, 2002)

37   W Churchill, *The Second World War: The gathering storm* (Houghton Mifflin, 1948)

38   D Bach, G Groesbeck, P Stapleton, R Sims, K Blickheuser and D Church, 'Clinical EFT (Emotional Freedom Techniques) improves multiple physiological markers of health', *Journal of Evidence-Based Integrative Medicine*, 24 (2019), https://doi.org/10.1177/2515690X18823691

39   DE McManus, 'Reiki is better than placebo and has broad potential as a complementary health therapy', *Journal of Evidence-Based Integrative Medicine*, 22/4 (2017), 1051–1057, https://doi.org/10.1177/2156587217728644

40   K Neff, Self-compassion: An alternative conceptualization of a healthy attitude toward oneself', *Self and Identity*, 2/2 (2003), 85–101, https://doi.org/10.1080/15298860309032

41   P Gilbert, *The Compassionate Mind* (Constable & Robinson, 2010) Ch6

42   M Hargrave, 'What does PDCA stand for in business? Plan-do-check-act cycle', *Investopedia* (30 November 2022), www.investopedia.com/terms/p/pdca-cycle.asp, accessed 4 October 2023

43   FB Gilbreth, *Popular Science* (December 1920), p34, https://libquotes.com/frank-bunker-gilbreth-sr/quote/lbu1a2n

44   M Evans, '23 and ½ hours: What is the single best thing we can do for our health?' (2011),

www.youtube.com/watch?v=aUaInS6HIGo,
accessed September 2023

45 DailyHealthPost Editorial, 'Neuroscience
Reveals: Gratitude literally rewires your brain to
be happier' (DailyHealthPost, 10 October 2020),
https://dailyhealthpost.com/gratitude-rewires-
brain-happier, accessed September 2023

46 L Carroll, *Alice's Adventures in Wonderland and
Through the Looking-Glass* (Macmillan Collector's
Library, 2016)

47 K Cavanaugh, 'Silly Olympics: Race for people
with no sense of direction' (2013), https://youtu.
be/15Z5nsyLDbE, accessed September 2023

48 S Dong, T Lin, JC Nieh and K Tan, 'Social signal
learning of the waggle dance in honey bees',
Science, 379/6636 (2023), 1015–1018, https://doi.
org/10.1126/science.ade1702

49 B Daisley, *Fortitude: The myth of resilience, and the
secrets of inner strength* (Penguin, 2023)

50 www.goodreads.com/quotes/92369-it-is-
in-changing-that-we-find-purpose, accessed
20 October 2023

51 TM Amabile and SJ Kramer, 'The power of
small wins', *Harvard Business Review* (May 2011),
https://hbr.org/2011/05/the-power-of-small-
wins

52 CG Jung, *Modern Man in Search of a Soul*
(Harcourt, Brace & World, 1933)

Further Reading

Dale, C and Peyton, P, *Physical Intelligence: Harness your body's untapped intelligence to achieve more, stress less and live more happily* (Simon & Schuster UK, 2019)

Feldman Barrett, L, *Seven and a Half Lessons about the Brain* (Picador, 2021)

Furr, N and Furr, SH, *The Upside of Uncertainty: A guide to finding possibility in the unknown* (Harvard Business Review Press, 2022)

Hamill, P, *Embodied Leadership: The somatic approach to developing your leadership* (Kogan Page, 2013)

Klein, G, *Seeing What Others Don't: The remarkable ways we gain insights* (Nicholas Brealey Publishing, 2017)

Yong, E, *An Immense World: How animal senses reveal the hidden realms around us* (Vintage, 2023)

Acknowledgements

I would like to express my sincere thanks to my amazing beta readers Chloe Brage, Linda Brage, Imogen Coggan, Emily Green, Jane Murray and Ash Schofield.

I am grateful also for the wonderful support and encouragement of family and friends; the team at Gail's in Farnham where I worked many hours on this book; my home, The Pilgrims, for holding me through the process; the London Writers' Salon whose Daily Writers' Hour kept me in my writing habit; Lily the cat for her beautiful and constant presence; and my gifted wellbeing team who accompanied me in looking after my body, spirit and mind during the most intense parts of the writing process.

Last, but not least, thank you to my publishing team at Rethink Press, especially Lucy, Joe, Anke and Kerry.

The Author

Amanda Muckalt stands for learning, flourishing and change.

By her mid-thirties, Amanda had lived in twenty homes across five cities and two continents; had six different careers; and set up her own leadership and life consulting business. Having now been a business owner for over twenty years, she balances change with stability. Amanda's understanding of business is rooted in chartered accountancy and corporate finance qualifications, and roles in audit, corporate finance and sales at KPMG. Her people-development skills have grown through teaching secondary school maths, leading a multicultural team of over thirty people in KPMG corporate finance, qualifying as a professional coach and working with executives one-to-one and in groups across a wide range of industry sectors, including professional, legal and financial services, pharmaceuticals, telecommunications, government and retail.

In her work with leaders, Amanda adopts a holistic approach and is passionate about supporting them to excel in change while flourishing in life. Her more conventional qualifications have been complemented with training courses in embodied leadership, conscious breathing, mindfulness-based stress reduction, Energetic NLP, Reiki, the Emotional Freedom Technique and spiritual direction. Yoga has been her beloved hobby for more than thirty years. Clients enjoy her down-to-earth style and positive energy.

Amanda has been a writer since she could hold a pen. As well as being a prolific journaler, she has blogged, published articles in *Accountancy Magazine, Finance & Management* and *Operations Management* and written several e-books for leaders on the themes of change, decision-making and flourishing. *The Stability Effect* is her first published book.

If you'd like to keep in touch or find out how Amanda can help you, your team or organisation, you can contact her in the following ways:

✉ amanda@centrefornewleadership.com

🌐 https://centrefornewleadership.com

🔗 www.linkedin.com/in/amandamuckalt